Ms. Cartwright

WE ALL HAVE A VOICE

MY MOTHER'S STORY

MAHA AL FAHIM

MAHA PUBLISHING

Copyright © 2014 Maha Al Fahim

All rights reserved. No part of this book may be reproduced in any form or by any means, electronic or mechanical, including photocopying, recording, or by an information storage and retrieval system—except by a reviewer who may quote brief passages in a review to be printed in a magazine, newspaper, or on-line—without permission in writing from the author.

Although the author and publisher have made every effort to ensure the accuracy and completeness of information contained in this book, we assume no responsibility for errors, inaccuracies, omissions, or any inconsistency herein.

Cover Design: Diane Feught

ISBN 978-0-9917576-1-9
Cataloguing data available from Library and Archives Canada
www.mothers-story.com
Maha Publishing

To my dear father and mother. Thank you for your support. Your encouragement and inspiration have helped me to blossom.

To my sweet sister, Fatima, and my amazing brother, Mohamed. Thank you for being the joy of my life.

Contents

	Prologue..	1
1	My Family...	5
2	The Long Wait..	15
3	Journey to the Holy City..................................	19
4	Feast Days with my Maternal Grandmother...	27
5	The New Maid..	31
6	Sultan's First Job...	35
7	A Secret Marriage..	41
8	A Sad Good-bye...	47
9	Light at the End of the Tunnel........................	51
10	Bright Days in Canada.....................................	59
11	A Family Tragedy...	63
12	Happy Days on the Oasis.................................	69
13	The Miracle..	73
14	The Man of God...	79
15	A Mixed Blessing..	83
16	Money Pouring from the Heavens..................	87
17	Dark Secrets...	93
18	The End of Sameera...	103
19	The Victims' Bait..	109
20	The Evidence Mounts.......................................	117
21	The End of Me..	121
22	The Devil is in the Fine Print..........................	125
23	Face to Face..	133
24	Farewell to my Homeland................................	139
	Epilogue..	149
	Glossary..	151

Prologue

Although this is a true story, I have changed the names of the characters to protect their privacy. My name and those of my mother and siblings remain the same.

For a number of years, I witnessed my mother in an acute state of depression. Her distress troubled me greatly but, as a child, I was too young to understand the complex reasons behind them. Finally, when I was 13, she was able to speak with me more openly about her troubles and her story began to unravel. It was then that she made the courageous decision to emerge from the lonely underworld of silence and to share her experience publicly – not just to bring meaning to her own suffering at the hands of her parents but also to redress the profound physical, mental, emotional, financial, and spiritual suffering of their countless victims. My mother's will to share this powerful account has been strong and unwavering, but her English skills are weak. And so she asked me to write her story on her behalf and to help her share it with the world.

Reliving some of her upsetting memories, as she had to do in order to tell me her story, often reduced my mother to tears and caused her to experience many nightmares. This was painful for both of us and yet, having committed ourselves to this path, we had no choice but to continue.

She told me of the difficult struggles she had to overcome, the dark secrets that she had discovered about her family, not all of which she could share with me, and the lessons that her harsh life has taught her. But this is not just her story. It is the story of the lost lives and harsh fates of thousands of others.

I know that sharing this story means exposing the misdeeds of people with whom I am related. I understand the importance of family loyalty but that will not weaken my resolve to do what is right. As a young woman of Middle East origins growing up in Canada in the 21st century, I also understand that the whole world is our family. Writing this book and directly experiencing my mother's lifelong suffering has shown me the terrible consequences of grieving in silence and the liberating power of speaking up against injustice. Through her story I learned that cultural taboos encage women in fear and shame, forcing them to silently struggle with injustice and to conceal their agony. We can no longer shut our eyes to their suffering. We can no longer block our ears from the truth. And we can no longer close our mouths from speaking that truth.

This book raises a number of important social justice abuses that festered in my mother's life for decades without being challenged. The violation of children and the denigration of women are the backdrop of my mother's story, as is the abuse of religion, the corrupting power of money, and the inflated importance given to one's social position and status in society. It is important to me and to my mother that these wrongs be explored, understood, and rectified.

My mother and I are all too aware that her story is shared by millions of others. The violence she faced reflects a greater atrocity. And her cries, long unheard, are echoed by millions of women and children all over the world. Within their unspoken suffering, they are buried alive. My desire to alleviate their oppression has helped me to find power in my pen and freedom in my words. The need for equality, the importance of education, and the liberating power of our voices, united as one, is the deeper message of this book.

> *For every child, woman and man,*
> *We are all one in Creation's command*
> *When we are lost in darkness, we seek for light*
> *When we are treated with injustice, we fight for our right*
> *For we are each born as people with dignity and pride,*
> *We will not die as victims who suffer and hide*
> *We all have a voice, to tell our stories*
> *We all have a choice, to share our memories*
> *I hope this book will inspire many more voices to rise*
> *To lead the world away from the path of deception and lies*
> *Together, we can lend a helping hand*
> *Together, in a stronger world we will stand.*

Where, after all, do universal human rights begin? In small places, close to home – so close and so small that they cannot be seen on any map of the world. Yet they are the world of the individual person...Unless these rights have meaning there, they have little meaning anywhere. Without concerted citizen action to uphold them close to home, we shall look in vain for progress in the larger world.

Eleanor Roosevelt,
Universal Declaration of Human Rights

CHAPTER 1

MY FAMILY

We think sometimes that poverty is only being hungry, naked and homeless. The poverty of being unwanted, unloved and uncared for is the greatest poverty.
— Mother Teresa of Calcutta

*A*llah Akbar, Allah Akbar, Allah Akbar. Every morning at 5:30, I would wake up to the beautiful call of mosque prayers declaring the glory of God. In the next room, I could hear my father, Hamad, reading the *Quran* while my mother, Fatana, whispered prayers.

My name is Amina and my story begins in the late 1970s in Dubai in the United Arab Emirates. I was nine years old at the time, the eldest of five children, and we lived with our parents in a small two-bedroom apartment on the top floor of a three-story building owned by my father. Every night I slept on a mattress on the floor with my three-year-old sister, Ghalia, while each of my three brothers who shared the room with us – Sultan, age seven, Rasheed, age five, and Mayed, age four – slept on his own single bed. Uncle Khaldoon, my father's younger brother, lived on the second floor with his family, and my maternal grandparents lived on the ground floor. Many of the other 15 apartments in the building were rented out to people of East Indian origin who worked for the government.

My paternal grandfather, father, and uncle owned a men's clothing shop in Ras Souk, an old, established public market in Dubai, where they sold goods imported from India and China. On the weekends, my parents would travel and sell their wares in other towns and cities in the Emirates, including Al Ain, Ras Al Khaimah, and Ajman. While they were away, I was responsible for the care of the younger children and the upkeep of the home, as I had been since I was seven years old. It was my job to feed my four siblings, teach them, keep them entertained, and stop my aggressive brothers from getting into fights. It was hard, tiring work, and the only thing that made it bearable was anticipating the delicious *shawarma* sandwich, a wonderful combination of juicy roasted beef, sour pickles and hummus, all rolled together in flat bread, which my parents brought back for us.

We would anxiously wait all day, half-starved because our cook didn't work weekends, until we would finally hear the door unlock at around 9 PM. We would rush to our parents excitedly, grabbing at the white plastic bag filled with our eagerly anticipated treats. Soon, all would be silent, as we each sat alone, enjoying every bite as though it were our last. Our parents never let us forget that, at 2Dhs (abbreviation for *dirhams*, United Arabic Emirates currency) per sandwich (i.e., about 55¢), such a treat was "very costly."

One weekend, I was very sick and struggling to do my duty and take care of my siblings. At three o'clock in the afternoon, I managed to scrounge up the ingredients to make them each a cheese sandwich, and then turned on the television and took out some toys from our little toy basket to keep them busy. Staggering to the couch, I dropped my dizzy head on a pillow and watched them play. I touched my forehead and realized that my fever was high. Even the cool breeze of the air conditioner could not cool me off. I tried desperately to keep my eyes open but it was impossible. Soon I fell into a deep sleep. Even though my brothers played very loudly, I could not hear a thing. Then a piercing shriek from Rasheed woke me up with a start. To my horror, I saw blood streaming down his face, covering his shirt in red.

"What happened to you?" I screamed. Then, out of the corner of my eye, I spotted my brother, Sultan, guiltily sitting in the corner.

"Sultan punched me in the nose!" Rasheed cried.

Concerned about Rasheed, I phoned my mother to get her advice. She angrily told me that she would call Uncle Khaldoon for help. This eased my worry somewhat and I did my best to stop Rasheed's nose from bleeding and to clean him up. About fifteen minutes later, there was a loud banging on our door. I unlocked it and there was Uncle Khaldoon, who was a younger version of my father – a big-bellied, round-faced man with a moustache and van dyke beard. I tried to explain to him what had happened when, without warning, he slapped my face so hard that I fell to the ground. A bright white light flashed before my eyes. My cheeks felt as though they were bleeding. I covered my face with my hands. Crying uncontrollably, I couldn't catch my breath. His hard hands left a mark on my cheeks and his harshness left a scar in my heart. Unremorseful, my uncle grabbed Rasheed's arm and dragged him down to the second floor. I guess he was furious that we were ruining his weekend with his family.

Married to Razya, an educated Indian woman, Uncle Khaldoon was always very kind to his five-year-old son and three-year-old daughter. I never saw him hit them. Unlike our apartment, theirs was filled with treats and toys, and every evening he would take his family out for smoothies, fresh juice, and ice cream. Then, a couple of hours later, we would hear his car horn beeping as though to announce that they had returned from their delightful adventure, whether it was dining at a restaurant, watching the latest movie at the cinema, or playing at an amusement park. While we tried to sleep in our dark and crowded bedroom, we could hear his children burst into happy laughter as they closed the car doors and entered their home. This always brought envy to our hearts. Unlike our parents, Uncle Khaldoon and Aunt Razya never left their children for days at a time to fend for themselves.

However, Uncle Khaldoon always treated us like street kids, referred to us as savages, and discouraged us from visiting his home. Whenever we knocked on his door, his maids refused to open it. Whenever we wanted to play with his children, he would not allow us, considering us dirty kids who would contaminate his darlings with our bad attitude. It seemed as though he took his cue from my parents, who didn't care the slightest bit about our feelings. I never understood why so many of the adults in our lives treated us in this way.

After my uncle stormed off with my crying brother, I waited in fear of what would happen when my parents returned home. I was especially afraid that my violent father would hit me, as he often did when he was angry. All my eagerness to see my parents arrive with the *shawarmas* disappeared. As the clock ticked mercilessly, I tried to come up with reasons to convince them that it was not all my fault, but fear and fever clouded my brain and I could not think clearly. After several fretful hours, I heard their key unlocking the front door. I ran to the kitchen and hid behind the door, peeking through the narrow gap anxiously. I was so relieved to see my father throw his exhausted body on the couch and turn on the local news channel, too tired to beat me.

However, when my mother entered the kitchen, she spotted me behind the door and began yelling at me.

"You are good for nothing. Why should we feed and take care of you?" I told her that Uncle Khaldoon beat me, hoping that she would feel sympathy for me, but no such luck.

"You deserved that! You're lucky Rasheed only got a bleeding nose. If he got hit in the eye and injured, you would have been responsible for that and sent to jail," she said angrily.

That really frightened me. I felt like a criminal. But after that incident, even though my parents sometimes went away for weeks, I learned to solve my problems on my own. In retrospect, I can see that this impossible challenge gave me the strength I would need to cope with the troubles that lay ahead.

Apart from separating Sultan from Rasheed, my other strategy was to invent games to entertain my siblings for the hours and days that they were in my care. One day, as I was wandering by the garbage bins outside our building, I spotted a large wooden board.

I picked it up, took it home and, after drawing roads and houses on it, I transformed it into a city for my brothers' toy cars. This kept them occupied for hours. And instead of trying to force them to take a bath, I told them, "Imagine the tub is the ocean, and this plastic water bottle is a ship!"

Time went by faster because I was having fun too. It was a good thing because soon my parents started visiting Afghanistan, India, Pakistan, Yemen, and other countries that were much farther away.

Despite the way she treated me, I yearned for my mother's love. A short, plump, dark-skinned woman with dark wavy hair, thick eyebrows and thin lips, she would brush away my hands whenever I tried to give her a hug. It was obvious that she didn't like me hugging her. However, she did like money and would do anything to get it. From the time I was very young, I noticed my mother's love for wealth. From day until night, in the bedroom or in the living room, I would overhear her suggesting to my father new ways of increasing their profits. She was my father's business companion and comptroller. Her suggestions were his actions. On their long business trips, she attended meetings with him, chose the store goods and negotiated the prices.

After her business dealings were done, she became a woman of leisure. Sometimes I would see her using a long silver key to unlock her huge safe, overloaded with sparkling diamonds and golden jewellery. I could see a spark of joy in her eyes that I never saw when she looked at me.

My father spent a great deal of money indulging my mother's every desire, but he did not waste a penny on his children. In fact, he beat us. Whether it was because we were too loud or because his day was not going well and he was simply angry, he would hurl plates, teacups, and metal toy cars at us. Since our apartment was small and we couldn't escape him, he would succeed in hitting his target, often drawing blood – and tears. At other times, he would lunge at us, yelling and red-faced, his hands clenched into powerful fists, craving to hit something. I would try to hide behind our bedroom door, desperately hoping that the darkness would hide and protect me, but he would always find me. All I could do was hug my knees, hide my head, and close my eyes tightly, hoping to lessen the impact of the painful punches coming at me, one after another. I would cry and cry, until finally my father felt too exhausted to beat me any longer.

Once he left the room, I would sit alone, pain throbbing throughout my body, which would be covered in large, dark bruises. Hot tears streamed down my cheeks. Believing that I had deserved his beatings, deep sorrow filled my soul. I had no tomorrow to look forward to because today, filled with fear and self-reproach, always repeated itself. I was in a tunnel of darkness with no hint of light, no one to ask me how I felt, no one to care about me. What was my purpose in a life that was such a nightmare? I wished that my eyes would close and never open again. And yet, I thought it was normal for a father to hit his children. Especially when I saw my mother silently watching.

Sometimes, feeling lonely and unwanted after my father's brutal beatings, I would run barefoot to my paternal grandmother's house. Despite being afraid of going outside alone, especially at night, the pain I felt inside kept me running and running to the only place where I felt loved. I would arrive breathlessly at her two-bedroom mud-brick house, push open the heavy wooden doors, and run to my grandmother's room, where she would often be praying. As soon as she was finished, I would give her a big hug and tell her I missed her. She would kiss my cheeks and tell me she missed me too, and then would ask me why I had come all that way alone.

At first I would complain that my father had beaten me, but after calming down, I would say that I had come to see her because I loved her. She would then call my mother to tell her that I was safe at her place. I would hear her demanding to know why I'd been beaten. Being with my grandmother made me feel like somebody cared about me.

After preparing a snack and getting me a soft drink, my grandmother would sit with me on the bedroom carpet, gently rubbing my back while I ate. Then I would ask her to tell me a story. She only had one story, the same one that her mother had told her at bedtime, the tale of the golden fish that had granted three wishes to a poor girl. Even though she told the same story again and again, each time I heard it felt like the first time.

My time with her was joyful – until my grandfather arrived home from work. He was a rough and stingy man. Despite his wealth, he only provided a small amount for household expenses, and so my grandmother had to work for a living. For as long as I could remember, she ran a small fabric business from her home. Her second room was filled with all types of fabrics. I loved feeling their diverse textures and admiring the bright colors, beautiful patterns, and sparkling sequins. Sometimes, I would grab pen and paper and sit on the floor to draw my favorite designs.

When her customers, who were mostly local ladies, came by, they would choose their fabrics and then chat with my grandmother, sipping the tea that she had prepared for them. My grandmother would listen while they talked about their personal lives, supporting them with their problems and congratulating them on their achievements. I loved it when the customers brought along their kids. We would play tic-tac-toe, hangman, and other simple games until it was time for them to leave.

Often one of the women would confide in my grandmother that she needed financial help. After listening to the woman's worries, she would go to her bedroom, get some money from her closet, roll it in tissue paper and place it in the woman's hands. Even though she did not have much money, she gave as much she could.

If it were up to me, I would have stayed there forever. But after a few days, I would hear my grandfather arguing with my grandmother, telling her that I was bothering him and invading his privacy. I would feel sad, yet I knew that it was time for me to leave. I also knew that my grandmother had no authority in her home and so, to avoid making her feel bad, I would tell her that I wanted to go home. She would reluctantly call my mother to come and pick me up. Before I left, she would give me a big hug to cheer me up. Sometimes she gave me toys, trinkets, or a box of chocolates to share with my siblings.

I couldn't wait until my next visit with her.

Chapter 2

THE LONG WAIT

We do, still, very much want our mothers to love us; indeed our mood, even our well-being, often depends on it.
- Victoria Secunda

Despite her lack of education and inability to read or write, my mother always wanted to present herself as a modern woman like my uncle's wife, Razya. She was very proud when, at age 28, she became one of the first women in Dubai to get a driver's license and my father bought her a gleaming white Mercedes sedan. Because we had a cook who prepared basic meals for us, she was able to be a woman of leisure, spending her days shopping, socializing with friends and relatives, and attending every party that she was invited to.

Since the school bus did not stop near our apartment, I depended on my mother to get me to and from school, which was one of the first girls' public schools in Dubai. Although my school day ended at 1:00 PM, she rarely picked me up before 3:00.

For the first hour, I played teacher-student games, scribbled on the blackboard and enjoyed the empty classroom with the few other remaining students. But, after 2:00, the school gates were locked and all of the other students had left for home. I had to stand outside and felt very lonely. My only companion was an Indian man standing to the right of the gate, selling candy to students and passersby. Seeing his mouth-watering collection of chocolates, lollipops, gummies, and cotton candy would remind me of how starved I was, not having eaten since my early morning breakfast of eggs and bread. I wasn't given spending money or a packed lunch and my stomach would ache from hunger.

The most frightening part of my day began after the candy seller packed up his things and left. My shoes could not protect my feet from the burning desert sands, and so I sat on the ground, afraid and alone. With temperatures as high as 45 degrees Celsius, my lips were parched and pearls of sweat rolled down my back. There were no trees to cool me off. Sometimes strangers would stare at me with unfriendly eyes, bringing fear to my heart. I had heard many scary stories of children being kidnapped or killed and never seen again.

Sometimes my mother was so late that I would give up and walk home by myself, shivering in fear. People rarely walked in Dubai, especially in the late 1970s. It was a city created for cars, with no pedestrian sidewalks or lighted crosswalks. If I were lucky and saw a woman walking on her own, I would rush to her side and walk with her so that I could feel safer.

Once when I arrived at our building, having walked home alone, I passed by my maternal grandmother's apartment on the ground floor. Looking through her window, I saw my mother drinking tea and chatting with my grandmother and some other ladies. I knocked on the window, which really annoyed my mother. She furiously cut short her conversation. When she opened the sliding glass window, I felt like I had just stepped into a refrigerator. I loved the air conditioner's cold breezy air blowing on my sweaty face.

"Why did you come? I was going to pick you up," she said irritably.

"But you were really late. They closed the school gates and everyone left. I felt lonely and scared."

"Don't you have patience? Wait! In the end, I will pick you up."

One day, I was waiting outside the school gates even longer than usual. Finally, after two hours, I was so hungry and tired that I set off for home. The sun was unbearably hot. Before crossing the four-lane road, my eyes squinting from the intense sunlight, I looked for cars, but didn't see any. I quickly ran across, looking over my right shoulder. Then I heard a deafening screeching noise approaching from the left. Turning to look, I saw a speeding car heading right toward me! My heart leapt in fear. Sweat poured down my face. Seeing certain death before my very eyes, I was so terrified that I was unable to move. There was nothing I could do but stand there and close my eyes tight, hoping death would not be painful.

A few seconds later, the screeching noise stopped. I opened my eyes to see the car right next to me. The driver lowered the window and yelled at me angrily, "Are you crazy? Why are you running on the streets?"

I didn't answer, I just ran. My heart was pounding and it was very difficult to breathe, but I ignored his yelling and kept on running. Despite the distance, I ran all the way home.

My father was sitting on the sofa with a tray of food on his lap, watching television. When he saw me, he said, "Good thing you are here. Your mother is attending her cousin's bridal shower. She called and said that she would be late."

I said nothing and ran to the kitchen to make myself a snack. I was too afraid to tell my father that my terrifying walk home might have been my last.

CHAPTER 3

JOURNEY TO THE HOLY CITY

You have set out to exchange one world for another - to gain a new world for yourself in exchange for an old one which you never really possessed.
— Muhammad Asad

One day, close to the end of my grade three academic year, my mother picked me up from school on time, which really pleased me. This was because we were traveling the 2000 km to Saudi Arabia for *Haj*, or pilgrimage to Mecca, the Holy City. My parents had often told me that it was each proper Muslim's duty to go on *Haj* at least once during his or her lifetime. I had heard people warn my parents that part of the long, endless road to Mecca was unfinished and there were few facilities such as gas stations, washrooms or restaurants along the way.

One person said to my father, "You have the money. You are the owner of an eighteen-suite building. You own a shop. Why don't you fly instead?"

But my father's answer was always the same, "If I make it through alive, I will save a lot of money. If I never make it back, I will die a religious hero."

Remembering these conversations brought trepidation to my first holy journey to Mecca.

The journey took two days. Sometimes we drove along two-lane roads. Other times, there was only one lane. The road was often bumpy with no streetlights along the way. At night, we slept outside on the dark desert, unprepared for the cold weather that chilled our bones and caused our teeth to chatter. My mother threw down a blanket for us to sleep on but it was no protection against the hard rocks that made for a painful night.

We often heard wild dogs barking and male camels fighting – a very scary sound. There were also snakes and scorpions, which really terrified us. I told my mother that the scorpions might sting us or the camels might step on us, but she said that nothing bad would happen because we were going to Mecca to worship God. As long as God was with us, nothing could harm us. The noise of the animals didn't stop me from admiring the beautiful stars twinkling like diamonds in the clear night sky. I longed for them to be real diamonds so that I could collect them and give them to my parents. Maybe then they would love me more. Soon, the black sky turned purple and then pink as the beautiful golden sun began to rise.

Folding up the blanket in the morning, I discovered a gift from Mother Nature lying on the desert floor. The stones that had brought pain to our backs looked like marbles in beautiful shades of pink, grey, black, and white. I gathered some up in a plastic bag and put them in my pocket. My mother opened a can of tuna and served it on flat bread. We each ate our small share, wondering if there would be more food later on.

We drove for hours and hours. We were all nauseated and tired and our bodies were cramped. My brothers fought incessantly. We were all sweating from the burning heat, yet my father did not turn on the air conditioning, not wanting the engine to get overheated. He opened the window instead, but the hot desert wind dried our throats, burned our faces, and hurt our ears. Rasheed and Mayed were so hungry they couldn't stop crying. My father kept telling us that we would get out at the next stop, but the next stop never came.

To entertain myself, I took out my newly gathered desert stones and admired their beauty. Then I used them to tell my siblings stories. That kept us all busy until the afternoon when we finally found a stop with a cafeteria, mosque and gas station.

While our car was getting refueled, we headed to the cafeteria. Many Indian road workers crowded the place, sitting and eating around long wooden tables. There were few choices for food, but we satisfied ourselves with a whole grilled chicken served with rice. We gobbled down our chicken, appreciating every bite, even though it was unseasoned.

Because there were no signs along the way, we often got lost. One night, as my father drove in complete darkness, the road got narrower and narrower until there was nothing left except for two small sandy roads in front of us. We were in the middle of nowhere and my father was getting more and more agitated, not knowing which road to take. He turned on the inside lights and looked at his map in confusion. Unfortunately, there was only one road marked on the map, not two. Looking out the window, we saw nothing but complete darkness. Wild dogs were howling.

After about an hour of waiting, my little brother Mayed started crying loudly. Then, miraculously, we saw two bright yellow lights approaching us from a distance. It was a Pakistani man riding a small tractor.

My father was very pleased to see him and quickly lowered his window, "We are going to Mecca. Which road do we take?" The man told him to take the road on the right and to drive for about 45 minutes until we reached the main street. My father took his advice and, before long, we arrived at a large mosque. My mother told us that we were close to Mecca and that we had to change our clothes.

We entered the mosque and bathed and changed our clothes in the washroom. My mother, Ghalia and I put on simple white dresses and covered our hair with white scarves. My father and brothers each wore an *ihram*, which consisted of two large white pieces of cloth, one covering them from waist to ankle and the other thrown over their shoulder. All of the pilgrims wore these white garments, which, in the Muslim faith, symbolize equality and unity before God.

We drove for two more hours and then saw a long line of tiny sparkling orange lights. We gasped in excitement. It seemed as though it had been forever since we had last seen city lights. The closer we got, the more our hearts pounded with happy anticipation.

When we reached Mecca, we saw many old buildings along the wide streets, which steadily became narrower and more crowded. Cars crawled alongside thousands of pilgrims, all headed in one direction – to *Masjid Al Haram*, the largest mosque in the world. Although we were not far away from the mosque, it took us a long time to get there and it took my father over an hour to find a place to park the car.

When we finally arrived, I looked up in amazement at this beautiful mosque, my heart feeling light as I entered it. We all removed our shoes and walked along the cold, white marble floors. I will always remember the majesty of that moment. Wherever I looked, bright spotlights lit up this holy place. Beautiful chandeliers illuminated huge pillars decorated with golden works of art. Some distance away, I saw thousands of pilgrims devoutly walking together around the *Kaaba*, "The Noble Cube," the symbol of unity for all Muslims around the globe. It does not matter where or when a Muslim prays, all of our prayers must be directed toward the *Kaaba*. We soon joined the other pilgrims and we too became a part of a large procession called the *Tawaf*.

Soon afterwards, we completed another pilgrimage near the *Kaaba*, at the *Safa Wal Marwa*, where we walked seven times along a lengthy tunnel between two small hills.

After we finished our spiritual duties for the day, my father took us to a nearby hotel where we stayed the night. The next morning, after eating a simple breakfast, we drove for four hours along the crowded streets of Saudi Arabia, until we reached a place called Arafa.

There, we prayed on the desert hills until sunset. It is believed that whoever prays on that very day will get their prayers answered. Tomorrow at sunrise would be our big celebration – *Eid Al Adha* or the Feast of Sacrifice.

After a second night at the hotel, we got up at 6:00 AM, dressed in new clothes, and headed for the *Eid* prayers in Mecca. My father and brothers sat in the men's area of the Haram, waiting with many other men for the *Salat al Eid* prayer. Ghalia and I sat in the women's area with my mother. A number of women were walking around with trays, baskets and bags, all full of sweets for the kids. Some of them came up to us and gave us some candies, which brought smiles to our faces. Other women presented the children with a *Riyal* (Saudi currency unit) as an *Eidiya*, or money gift, as a way of sharing their blessings and happiness.

Later, as night set in, we drove some more until we arrived at another place called Mona. From the distance, we could see thousands of white tents covering the desert grounds. We rented a tent and stayed there and worshipped for three days. That was the end of our religious duties. After this phase of the holy journey, most Muslims would return home – but not us.

Hours of driving awaited us as we returned to the Holy City. Finally, we reached an old building in an old neighborhood. My father unlocked the door to an empty two-bedroom apartment with nothing but a few mattresses inside.

"This is where we will be staying for the next couple of weeks."

Exhausted, we dropped onto the mattress and, before we knew it, we were fast asleep. The following afternoon, we awoke to a sweet aroma coming from the small kitchen. Our eyes opened to see our mother preparing us some lentils. I helped her serve the food and we all sat together on the floor to enjoy the meal.

That was when my father said, "Now we have to go to the mosque for prayers, but because the way is very long and tiring, you will stay at home."

For days thereafter, they left the house in the

afternoon and locked the door behind them, not to return until later in the evening, often with several bags in their hands. I watched as my mother emptied them. There were *prayer beads, prayer rugs,* necklaces with pendants depicting the *Kaaba,* and several other souvenirs. My mother packed them away to give out as gifts or to sell as goods in my father's store.

At first we were content to stay in the apartment because we felt settled after hours and hours in the car. But as the days crawled by, we became more and more bored. There was no television, no games, no entertainment of any kind. There was nothing to do but wait for the day when our parents would take us home.

Fear started to creep into my thoughts. What about school? What about all the days I've been absent? What about all the tests I've missed?

I said to my mother, "We have finished our duties here. When are we going to go back to Dubai? I am afraid I will get behind in my schoolwork."

Her reply did nothing to alleviate my worries: "We came all the way to Mecca. We cannot just go back all of a sudden. We are here to pray and to get closer to God. So we should make the most out of our time."

After four endless weeks, when we finally returned home, the school year was finished and I had missed all of my final exams. I was devastated to get a failing grade. I felt like a hopeless failure and couldn't hold my head up. If anyone asked how I did on my exams, I would tell them that I had not yet picked up my report card.

My father did not care about my grades and my mother blamed me for being irresponsible. "Don't make excuses that you went to Mecca! You yourself were foolish from the start. If you did well at the beginning of the year, you wouldn't have failed."

Her comments made me feel even worse but they also made me realize something. This was my life. My future was my responsibility. I needed to think for myself rather than follow my parents' views on education. I promised my family that I would study harder next year and I refused to go anywhere during the final exams. The following year, when my parents, siblings and beloved paternal grandmother left for Saudi Arabia, I stayed with my maternal grandmother, who disliked me as much as my mother did.

I had no other choice.

CHAPTER 4

FEAST DAYS WITH MY MATERNAL GRANDMOTHER

It is hard, she thought, it is hard for us to think of people who dislike us because none of us, in our heart, believes that we deserve the hatred of others.
— Alexander McCall Smith

My maternal grandmother, who was in her early fifties, was an older version of my mother. Whenever we visited her in her apartment, where she lived with my grandfather, she just looked annoyed. She particularly disliked seeing us at mealtime. If we dared to reach into her fruit basket for something to eat, she grabbed the food out of our hands and cursed us.

"May God shred you apart," or "May you die and never see any goodness in your life." We didn't know why she hated us so much but we knew enough to stay out of her way.

However, she never uttered a single bad word to us in front of my mother. She had a forked tongue and two faces. Whenever guests visited her house, she treated them with respect and kindness. She served them with sweet flattery. But once they were out of sight, she cursed and insulted them. When I was small, I found it hard to understand how these two faces could belong to the same person. It seemed to me that her heart was always consumed by hatred and envy.

I wasn't looking forward to staying with her and for good reason. From the moment I set foot on her doorstep, she told me I was a pain in the neck and demanded to know why I didn't go with my parents instead of staying with her. She called me the most obscene names, some of which I didn't understand until I got older. But from the way that she said them, I knew that they were offensive. She kept track of every bit of food I put into my mouth, counting the money that I was costing her. I tried to please her by cleaning the house, washing the dishes, or giving her a massage, but she didn't appreciate my efforts. I counted the days until I could leave her house. Every minute there felt like an hour.

During *Eid Al Adha*, a time when people visited one another, wore beautiful new clothes, and feasted with their families, we spent almost every single day in the house. When I tried to watch television, she would demand that I turn it off because I was wasting electricity.

When I studied at night, she would turn off the lights and say, "If you want to study, use daylight not my house lights."

I often cried at night in my small dark room, looking out through the window where I could see the other kids playing and enjoying themselves with their families. Their laughter was more than I could bear.

I had to remind myself that my grandmother provided me with a place to stay, even if it wasn't all that pleasant. I hadn't gone there to play or to have fun. I had gone there to study. I dreamt of being a doctor when I grew up, hoping that would make my parents proud of me. I believed that very hour of study would take me one step closer to making this dream a reality.

My hard work rewarded me with an "A" on my grade three final exams. Something inside me brightened up. Feeling in control of my education and of my destiny gave me strength and optimism.

CHAPTER 5

THE NEW MAID

If you want to keep a secret, you must also hide it from yourself.
- George Orwell

By the time I turned 14, it seemed as though the world was smiling upon us. My father had become a wealthy man and now owned three stores. My mother had given birth to another son, Mahmoud. We had moved from our two-bedroom apartment into a four-bedroom house with a yard. I only had to share a room with Ghalia, not my noisy brothers, and I slept in a bed for the first time in my life. Even better, we got fewer beatings. The house was a lot bigger, we had more space to run and hide, and our father could not easily catch us. Also, the bus stopped by our house, so I didn't have to rely on my mother to get me to and from school. Moreover, the Ministry of Education provided lunch, for which I was very grateful.

With my father's businesses expanding, my mother's life had become busier. When she wasn't assisting my father on his business trips or helping to design their new building in the center of the city, she led an active social life with relatives and friends.

My life, on the other hand, was quiet. On weekdays, I went to school in the morning, did housework in the afternoons, and did homework in the evenings. I loved the weekends and spent my free time sewing clothes, making accessories, and reading. I would often read psychology books that I bought from book fairs or borrowed from the public library. I wanted to better understand my parents. Why did my father beat us? Why didn't my mother show any care or concern for us? If they had been well educated, would they have treated us the same way? Why were they so afraid that they would be poor when they were so wealthy? I read many books but did not find a single answer to these questions.

My free time increased when my parents hired Malla, a Muslim maid in her mid-twenties from the Philippines. She was short and so thin that her collarbones stuck out. She wore a long dress and covered her hair with a scarf, called a *hijab*. I was happy to have her clean the house, wash the dishes and do the laundry instead of me.

Unfortunately, after about a year, she abruptly left for the Philippines and never came back. Worried, I asked my mother what had happened, but all she would say was that Malla had to return to attend to her sick father.

Once again, a huge weight was back on my shoulders as I struggled to juggle schoolwork with the upkeep of an eight-person household. It took my parents seven months to get a new maid. This time, they did not care about her religion, but they insisted on hiring a married woman with children, which was not easy to find.

One day when I was cleaning my parents' bathroom, I found out why they were so particular about their maid's marital status. There, in the garbage can, was a torn envelope with a torn picture inside it. Curious to find out whose picture it was, I assembled the torn pieces to reveal a baby boy wearing a blue cap. He looked as though he was about two months old. Then I read the letter that accompanied it and was shocked at what I learned.

The letter, which was from Malla, said that her family was enraged at her for getting pregnant, that she didn't have enough money to raise her child, and that she needed my parents to provide financial support.

"After all he is your grandchild as well."

She asked how Sultan, now 16, was doing and said that when her son grew up, she would tell him that Sultan was his father. I stared at the letter in horror and the hair on my arms stood on end. Without a thought, I threw the letter in the garbage and immediately took out the trash.

I felt pity for Malla. But mostly, my heart went out to her child. How would she be able to feed him, if she couldn't afford it? How would he survive in this world without an identity or family name? And how would he live without a family that wanted him?

It didn't appear as though my parents and Sultan took any responsibility for him and there was nothing I could do about it. I was afraid that if I said anything, I would be beaten and thrown out of the house. Being abandoned was a constant fear because whenever I spoke up about anything, my parents would tell me, "If you do not like it, leave."

So I tried to do the impossible. I tried to forget.

CHAPTER 6

SULTAN'S FIRST JOB

Do not fall prey to the false belief that mastery and domination are synonymous with manliness.
— Kent Nerburn

One afternoon, I saw Sultan coming home from school looking miserable. When my father asked him what was wrong, my brother took his grade 9 mid-term report card out of his backpack and handed it to him. My father unfolded it and stared at it for some time, and discovered that Sultan had failed all of his courses.

Sultan looked nervous, no doubt remembering what had happened when he had failed the second grade. My father had gotten very angry, had said that he was wasting his money on a private school education that went nowhere, and had insisted that Sultan attend public school instead. Thereafter, none of my brothers attended private schools.

Sultan agitatedly blurted out an excuse: "It is not my fault! Blame our teachers! How do they expect us to know what the answer is if they never taught it to us!"

This time, my father did not get angry and instead said, "Don't worry, education is not important. We already have lots of money. You can work in one of our stores and you can make these people who finish university your servants. The amount of money they make in one month, we can make in one day!"

From tomorrow on, Sultan would be the manager of my father's biggest and most modern store, which specialized in Men's undergarments. My mother was very proud of him. Her son was a man now.

For the first couple of months, Sultan worked hard. Following up on a suggestion put forth by one of his employees, he recommended to my father that he sell stationery instead, explaining that, with the large number of new public and private schools in the city, there was a lot of demand for this merchandise. My father agreed, their new stationery store thrived, and their profits grew.

Sultan seemed to be one of those people who did poorly in school but who was successful in business. He soon earned my parents' trust and confidence and my father turned his attention to managing his other stores and buildings. My parents were so proud of Sultan's ability to manage the store that they bought him a new car. It wasn't just any car. It was a late model black Mercedes sedan.

As soon as he got his car, Sultan began returning home later and later. One night, when he got in at 2:00 in the morning, my mother asked him why he was so late. Sultan explained that, because it was *Ramadan*, people fasted in the daytime and shopped at night, which meant that he had to keep the store open later than usual.

During *Ramadan*, people fasted from sunrise to sunset for one whole month in order to better empathize with the poor. It was a time when people tried to get closer to God and to renounce egocentrism. They would also commit to helping the needy. I tried to embrace the spirit of this sacred time by putting my sewing skills to good use. *Ramadan* was one of those rare times when I was able to visit the clothing stores in the neighborhood where my father's stores were, something that he would otherwise discourage me from doing. I would go at a prearranged time and pick up the stores' unwanted, stained or damaged children's clothing. I would then go home and work for long hours, washing, stitching, decorating, and ironing – transforming them from unwanted to wonderful.

Then I would gift-wrap them with beautiful paper and ribbon and, a few days before *Eid al-Fitr*, I would distribute them to the children of poor families. I wanted them to have something beautiful to wear during the celebration, so they wouldn't feel left out. Seeing their infectious smiles inspired me to do the same thing every year.

One Monday afternoon, while collecting clothing from one of the stores, I saw an enormous crowd of people at Sultan's store. Impressed by his success, I decided to go and congratulate him. There were several women there. Some were older women who wore the *niqab*, a black cloth that covered the face, but displayed the eyes. There were also many young Asian women. I saw Sultan sitting in his big black leather office chair behind his large gleaming desk. On either side of him were two serious-looking Indian employees, standing with their arms crossed as though they were his bodyguards.

Sultan was spinning his chair around and chatting up the young women. As soon as he saw me, however, he ran up to me angrily, demanding to know what the hell

I was doing there. I told him that I was just stopping by to congratulate him on his success. Instead of thanking me, he pushed me out of his store and told me to go home.

When I got out, an employee from the store next door was sitting on a wooden box, working a toothpick between the gaps of his teeth. I asked him if he knew what was going on and he laughed derisively. He told me that every Monday after the noon-hour prayers, local old women gathered at Sultan's store to ask him for help. He would give each of them 500 Dhs, provided they first gave him some blessings and called him Sheikh Sultan. Not only that, but every night Sultan went to the bar with his employees and female admirers and would spend an average of five thousand Dhs. I asked the gentleman how he knew this and he replied that Sultan's employees had told him.

I said that I was worried that the store would go bankrupt, which the man didn't dispute. Although the store had been very profitable, Sultan didn't know how to handle such a large amount of money.

He also bribed his employees to tell our father, "Master Hamad," that everything was going great. Sultan warned them that if they ever told Master Hamad the truth, he would fire them.

I went home to tell my mother what I had discovered.

After a short, anxious pause, she dismissed me by saying, "First of all, who gave you permission to go to his store? You know Sultan's business is prospering well, but you just have an evil heart. You want to ruin his reputation because you are like the salty sea – bitter and jealous! Even if he burned all the money, it's his money."

After that day, I understood that my mother valued her son as much as she valued her money. Apart from the prestige of having sons, she wanted to be able to brag that the boy she had raised (and whose face resembled hers) was qualified for this responsible job. In the circles in which my mother travelled, when a woman wanted to boast in front of her husband, she would brag about raising a lion's cub. My mother had four cubs to boast about and she wasn't about to jeopardize that. Anything that made my brothers look bad would make her look bad and so nothing I said had any impact on her. I decided to remain quiet and let time do its work.

Ramadan came to an end, but Sultan's habit of arriving home late continued. This time he explained that his business was getting bigger and better and he had to work longer and harder. Gradually, as the months slipped by, my parents' doubts grew.

At the end of the year, when my father audited Sultan's accounts, he finally discovered the truth – the store had lost two million Dhs (about $550,000). This meant that bankruptcy was inevitable and therefore my father had to shut the store down. He was angry and disappointed at first, but the next day at dinnertime he told Sultan that it wasn't entirely his fault. It was also the employees' fault for taking advantage of him because of his youth. My father said that my brother did not need to worry because the construction of his new residential building would be complete in two months time. It would be a safer and more prestigious place for Sultan to work.

Obviously my mother had succeeded in calming my father down.

CHAPTER 7

A SECRET MARRIAGE

Nothing is more necessary or stronger in us than rebellion.
— Georges Bataille

Three years passed, during which Sultan successfully managed my father's new building. He also became more and more overweight, just like my father. My mother, however, was very proud of him and started looking for a beautiful woman for him to marry.

It is customary for the groom's family to gift the bride's family with money for the wedding, but my proud, ambitious mother wanted to offer far more than that. If she saw a stunning diamond sparkling behind a glass showcase in a store window, she would imagine the glamorous jewel around her future daughter-in-law's neck. Without concern for the cost, she would buy it as a gift for Sultan's future wife. Before long, she had bought her future daughter-in-law a stunning collection of rubies, emeralds, sapphires, diamonds, white gold, and much more. Her large coffer looked like a treasure box.

At social gatherings, I often heard her brag about presenting her successful son to his fashionable future wife. Then she would proudly open up her treasure box and display each piece to her group of admirers. She talked about the elaborate wedding at a five-star hotel that she would arrange for him and his beautiful bride. My mother wanted nothing more than for people to be in awe of her wealth, to envy her status, and to feed her desire for attention.

Then one afternoon our maid presented my mother with a white plastic bag hidden in the corner of the trunk of Sultan's car, which she had been cleaning. My mother quickly opened the bag and discovered a woman's brown print dress inside. It didn't belong to anyone in our family and she questioned Sultan about it. He behaved as though he had no idea how the dress got there, but I could tell that my mother didn't believe him.

That evening, after my father returned from work, my parents and Sultan went into the master bedroom, locked the door and started arguing. My other brothers and I eavesdropped and heard Sultan vowing on the *Quran* that he had no idea whose dress it was. In fact he was swearing so fervently that I believed he was innocent. My parents however, were suspicious. The arguing lasted so long that my other brothers and I got tired of listening and got on with our own lives.

After about two hours, the door to the master bedroom opened. I had never seen my mother look so angry and disappointed. My father was furious as well, but less so than my mother. Unlike what had happened with Malla, hiding the truth was not an option and so our father angrily informed us that Sultan had been secretly married for six months to a woman from Sri Lanka.

He then looked at Sultan and said, "When you get

bored with this woman, I want you to divorce her and get rid of her as soon as possible, as though nothing has happened. Do you understand?"

He gave them a small apartment and ordered Sultan to keep her there. Under no circumstances would she be living with us. However, Sultan was determined to introduce her to his family. Finally, after a few weeks of continuous pressure, my mother agreed to allow his wife to come for a visit. Like all of us, she was curious about what her son's wife was like.

We all imagined her to be a young gorgeous woman with whom my brother could not resist falling in love. However, we were surprised to see that his dark-haired, dark-skinned wife was short and squat with small beady eyes and a double chin. She was at least ten years older than Sultan and lacked the slightest hint of beauty.

Out of all of the women whom he could have chosen, it didn't make sense that Sultan would choose an unattractive older woman from a different culture. Although I doubted that their marriage stood on solid ground, I had to assume that Sultan saw something in this woman that made him want to marry her. He told us that he had changed her name from Selvakumari to Sameera, an Arabic name. He also told us that he had wonderful news: Sameera was pregnant!

My mother looked as though someone had dropped a bomb on her head.

However, the next day she began preparing a room for her new daughter-in-law and grandchild. It seemed as though she had accepted the situation. She announced to our close and extended family that her son had just gotten married and invited them to a small party at our place. I overheard many of our relatives scorning Sultan and making fun of his wife.

"Not only is she from Sri Lanka, but she is also very old."

"Why did he have to go all the way to Sri Lanka to find a wife? Had all of the local women disappeared?"

But my mother boldly declared, "Sameera is from a very wealthy and famous family in Sri Lanka. Her sister even got married to a wealthy Emirati general with an excellent service record."

My mother would stand up for her first daughter-in-law even if she had to lie.

After a few months, Sameera gave birth to a baby boy whom she and Sultan named Hamad to please my father. Gradually my parents accepted Sameera as a member of the family. I saw my mother playing with little Hamad and giving Sameera some of the jewels and clothes that she had collected. She also gave her a yellow-gold Rolex watch, a set of white-gold diamonds and an evening gown, hoping that these adornments would increase Sameera's prestige. I taught my new sister-in-law some useful Arabic words and explained to her some of our customs and traditions.

Meanwhile, my father's business was prospering rapidly. He built several additional residential and office buildings as well as a shopping mall. He also bought a country estate along the highway between Al Ain and Dubai. We began spending every weekend there.

When people asked my father the secret to his rapid prosperity, he would tell them that during the war between Kuwait and Iraq in the early 1990s, the prices of real estate dropped and he seized the opportunity to buy many pieces of well-situated commercial property at reduced prices. He started building his first 32-story tower on Sheikh Zayed Street, the most prominent location in Dubai. He dreamt of many glamorous skyscrapers rising to the clouds, all inscribed with his name.

My mother, on the other hand, told people that their good fortune had come from Sameera, thus hoping to cast her first daughter-in-law in a more positive light. She believed that anything belonging to one of her sons had to be displayed in the most grandiose manner possible.

CHAPTER 8

A SAD GOOD-BYE

You will lose someone you can't live without, and your heart will be badly broken, and the bad news is that you never completely get over the loss of your beloved. But this is also the good news. They live forever in your broken heart that doesn't seal back up. And you come through.
- Anne Lamott

I finished school at age 19. I had once wanted to please my parents by becoming a doctor, but I felt more comfortable in business than in science. Thanks to a scholarship awarded by the UAE Ministry of Education, I began studying business administration at Beirut Arab University.

Our house was a quieter place now that my parents were busy with their new tower, meeting with the engineers and working on the design. My mother had to make sure that their private tower reflected her personal touch. One day, I accompanied my parents on their daily tour of their new project. As soon as the workers saw my father's car, they ran up and surrounded it. When my parents opened their car doors, enthusiastic greetings awaited them. The foreman gave my mother a yellow engineer's hardhat, which she wore with pride. She relished walking around the site, followed by construction workers, all of them attending to her demands. At one point, I saw her unzip her purse and give out five Dhs to each of the workers.

When my father came over, she rushed to him and said, "Good thing I was here to show them their mistake. Otherwise, our building would have been ruined. The engineer felt ashamed because I knew more than him."

My father believed that his wife, whom they called, "Engineer Fatana," was a smart and popular woman.

My life was busy as well, studying and doing assignments for my university courses and helping my siblings with their homework. The best part of my day was the afternoon because that was when I went to visit my paternal grandmother.

Whenever I arrived, she would always tell me, "You arrived at the right time. Now let me make us some chai."

While she was busy in the kitchen, I visited with her beautiful, bright green parrot, a gift from one of her customers. I fed him peanuts and he held each peanut with his foot, while cracking it with its beak. Afterwards, he would say, "Hello, hello."

My grandmother and I would sit together, slowly sipping our tea while she shared some of her lessons about life. Then she would head back to the kitchen to cook dinner. She was very skilled at making different types of bread, all delicious. My favorite was paratha, a wonderful flatbread. I would watch my grandmother's hands quickly kneading the dough, and heating it on her steel tawa, or circular roti pan, over her small gas stove. While the dough cooked, she brushed it with oil and sprinkle on some sesame seeds. Then she would give it to me, fresh and hot. After I had finished eating, I would kiss her good-bye and leave before my grandfather arrived.

One weekend afternoon, she and her daughter Munira came for a visit. We sat in the living room and Aunt Munira put a large, dark green velvet jewellery box in my lap and said, "This is for you."

I opened it and found a long, heavy gold necklace. Hanging from it was a crescent moon with a natural pearl in the center. Many small gold coins hung on the sides of its chain. I looked at it in amazement as my grandmother told me that it was a gift for my wedding day.

"I bought this a long time ago, for your wedding day, but I fear I am not going to live to see the day you marry. I want you to have this in advance, so you will remember me."

My eyes filled with tears as I hugged and thanked her.

"I do not need a necklace to remember you. No matter what, you will live in my heart forever."

A month later, it was *Ramadan*. Usually, after the night prayers, families visited one another. One of these evenings, my parents and I were at my paternal grandparents' house. We were all chatting and having a good time. Too soon, my parents told me it was time to leave. As we parted, my grandmother held onto my hands, not wanting to let go.

"Please stay with me longer," she pleaded.

I said, "This is my final academic year, so I have to study tonight. I promise I will come tomorrow."

At about 3:00 every morning during *Ramadan*, all Muslim families wake up before dawn breaks in the sky and have *suhoor*, their morning meal. As we finished our *suhoor*, our phone rang.

My father answered the call and, with a stricken look on his face, told us, "It is my father. He thinks my mother is dead."

It couldn't be true! It had to be a nightmare. We rushed to their home, and there was my beloved grandmother, lying on the floor with her prayer shawl close by as always. Uncle Khaldoon, and Aunt Munira were also there, and the paramedics soon followed.

I stood in shock, tears streaming down my face, not wanting to believe she was gone. Two paramedics shoved their way to my grandmother and, using a defibrillator, tried to revive her.

"Sorry," they told us, "She has died of a heart attack."

Everyone was upset, especially Aunt Munira, who wailed in sorrow. I heard a cry of grief, and then realized that it was coming from me. I saw a picture of myself hanging on her wall. I prayed that God would take her to heaven and I wished that she had taken me with her. I cried and cried.

Without her, I had nothing left in this world. She was my mother, my friend, and my mentor. She was everything I had, and now she was gone.

Chapter 9

LIGHT AT THE END OF THE TUNNEL

One word frees us of all the weight and pain of life. That word is love.
- Sophocles

After my grandmother's death, I threw myself into my studies and, at age 23, I graduated from the Beirut Arab University with a Bachelor of Arts in Business Administration. I was proud of my work, but as far as my parents were concerned, it wasn't much of an accomplishment. Every time I prayed to God, I asked for an educated husband. I had suffered a lot from my uneducated parents and did not want my children to suffer the same fate.

One evening, my mother got a call from Malaka, a distant cousin, who told her that she had seen me at a wedding a few weeks ago and thought that I would be a suitable wife for her brother. In our culture, it is the young man's mother or sister's responsibility to select the woman whom they believe is suitable for him to marry. She wanted to schedule an appointment so I could meet them.

After the call, my mother told me the great news. In our tradition, the meetings always take place in the future bride's house so that prospective in-laws could see where the young woman had grown up and could learn more about her background.

However, my mother told me that she did not want to have the meeting at our house. She thought it would be better if we met them in one of my father's offices so that we would not have to prepare a feast as tradition required. She didn't want to waste her time or money on a marriage that she thought might not even happen.

A few days later, the meeting took place at my father's office. It was my first time meeting my future sister-in-law, Malaka, along with her brother, my prospective husband.

My mother welcomed them in and said, "I am very sorry this meeting did not take place in our house. You see we are expecting guests."

When I saw my future husband, I could tell that he was a respectable gentleman. He asked questions such as how old I was, what I had studied, what my hobbies were, if I knew how to cook, what my favorite book was, if I had any medical issues, etc.

I tried my best to answer him honestly. From the way he looked at me, he seemed to like me. Too shy to ask him many questions, the only thing I asked was what he was studying. After they left, I asked my mother's opinion about him.

"I don't care," she snapped, "The only thing I am going to tell you is that once you get married, whatever happens to you is your own responsibility."

I couldn't help but feel hurt. First, she had not let the meeting take place in our house as was customary, and now she refused to give me her opinion and support as any loving mother would.

"I never asked you for help before, but I need your help now more than ever. So why are you turning your back on me? You are my mother and your words are my path to the future."

She did not respond. When other girls get married, their mothers cry tears of happiness and support their daughters all the way. But my mother did not seem to have any feelings toward me. So I turned for help to my father's only sister, my Aunt Munira. I asked her to gather information from our relatives about my prospective husband.

One afternoon a few days later, Aunt Munira called and asked me to come over. Excited, I dropped everything to go and see her. She welcomed me with a warm smile and then led me to her living room, where I saw a steaming pot of chai and a plate of delicious chicken *samboosa*, which she had prepared in advance. She poured me some tea and offered some information about my potential husband.

She said that he was a highly educated man from a noble family, the ideal husband for me. She had no doubt that if I married him, I would have a peaceful life full of happiness.

"He is your light at the end of the tunnel."

I thanked my Aunt Munira profusely, but she warned me not to be too overjoyed. I still had to wait for him to approve the marriage.

After a few days, Malaka called, informing us that her brother had accepted the marriage. He had to travel to Canada to complete his PhD and so she scheduled an appointment for his family to bring us the money for our wedding.

The day that they arrived, I peeked through the living room door, waiting until most of my future husband's close family had sat down.

I saw seven women, one of whom was older than the rest. I assumed her to be my future mother-in-law. Most of them wore long sequined dresses that peeked through their simple, black cloaks, called *abayas*. One of the women had a big bouquet of flowers and another carried a tray of chocolates. The woman next to her held a small gold-colored suitcase. Also present was my aunt Munira, my maternal grandmother, my mother and some of my cousins.

Taking a deep breath, I slowly entered the room. I had chosen to wear a bright green dress with a green scarf, as I believed that green was my lucky color. I warmly greeted the guests and sat down beside my future mother-in-law. She was in her mid-sixties, yet she sat upright, looking confident and dignified. I was especially eager to make a good first impression on her.

She looked at me thoughtfully and asked, "Do you speak any languages other than Arabic?"

I replied that I also spoke English, Farsi, and Urdu. She smiled in response. I could tell that she was impressed. She then turned toward my mother.

"We are here to ask for your daughter to be my son's wife."

"We will be delighted to accept," my mother said.

My future mother in-law hugged me and congratulated me on the forthcoming marriage. All of my other relatives followed suit. My heart was so full that it seemed as though the air itself was filled with delight.

"Please come join our feast," my mother said, gesturing to the dining table, which was covered with delicious local food made by our cook.

There were gleaming silver plates heaped with warm long-grain rice, garnished with saffron, mixed herbs and fried onions. There was a whole roasted lamb, a large dish of *harees*, and another of grilled kabobs. There was also hummus and a large selection of salads. After enjoying the delicious first course in our dining room, we went to the living room for dessert. I served Arabian coffee and *baklava*, along with *basbousa*, a cake made from semolina, soaked in syrup.

After everyone left, I was so relieved that everything had gone well. It was a magical day for me. However, my mother immediately opened the gold-colored suitcase and, after counting the money, her face changed from eager to angry.

"They want us to arrange a beautiful wedding and this is the only money they brought! That is not enough!"

I counted the money as well and told her it was enough for a great wedding. It would cover the hotel reservation, meals, the stage, the band, my wedding dress and accessories, invitations and much more. But my mother was unsatisfied. My second cousin had received half a million *dirhams*. My other cousin had been given four hundred thousand *dirhams* along with a diamond set and a Rolex watch.

"Tomorrow someone will ask how much your groom's family offered us. I will be ashamed to tell them the truth. People will say that this amount reflects our class and image."

She insisted on calling Malaka to demand more money. I was determined to stop her. I told her that some people spent a fortune on their wedding, even taking out an uncomfortably large loan from the bank just to look glamorous and rich in other people's eyes. I did not want my life to be ruled by others' opinions. I wanted to live for myself. I didn't care about the money. I just cared about having a good husband. A wedding would just last a few days, but a good husband would be with me forever. None of this persuaded my mother but, surprisingly, my father agreed with me. He told my mother to make the most of the money that they had given us.

Three months later, we had arranged a wonderful wedding. A few days before the big day, my husband and his family, along with the *Mullah*, all arrived at our house to make our marriage official. The wedding itself lasted for two days.

On the first day, we had a smaller event, called *Laylat al hina* or Henna Night, for our immediate families. I sat on a mattress with matching pillows covered with green silk decorated with flowers made of gold embroidery and sequins. I wore the large gold necklace given to me by my paternal grandmother, along with long dangling earrings. An Indian lady decorated my hands with henna. Young girls from both of our families danced for us in their long colored dresses, bedecked with shining crystals. Meanwhile others were enjoying the delicious food and entertainment. The celebration continued until after midnight.

Our second night was the big night. This was the first wedding in our family and even my mother was excited. She wore a gold lace dress and stood at the front door, welcoming our guests and enjoying the attention she was receiving as the bride's mother. Once all 700 female guests were seated, I made my grand entrance. In front of me was a belly dancer wearing a candelabra crown on her head. Wearing a white lace gown, I walked down the aisle and sat on a long bench decorated with green leaves and fresh peach-colored flowers.

Meanwhile, in another room in the hotel, the groom and all of his male guests enjoyed their own celebration. After hours of dance performances, meals and music, my husband-to-be and his family entered the room. I felt incredibly happy to see him. He sat beside me while our guests shook our hands, extended their blessings and said good-bye. This was the most memorable moment of my life, a night full of happiness, celebration and love. A night that I will forever treasure.

After the wedding, we had a small party at my parents' home. There my new in-laws gifted me with jewellery, including gold belts, gold necklaces and rings. Now I had my own collection.

Two days later, we flew to Canada. My husband had to continue his graduate studies, so we didn't have a honeymoon. But the beautiful land of Canada was itself a place of dreams. I was full of eagerness and joy for our life ahead.

Chapter 10

BRIGHT DAYS IN CANADA

A house is made of walls and beams; a home is built with love and dreams.
- Dr. William A. Ward

Vancouver was lovely and green, the people were polite and friendly, and I enjoyed more privacy than I'd ever experienced in my life. But with my husband away working all day until late in the evening, I often felt depressed, lonely and homesick. Nevertheless, a year later, God blessed me with a beautiful baby girl whom we named Fatima. She brightened my life during those grey, cloudy days.

We rented a small one-bedroom apartment in a large, crowded residential complex in North Vancouver. We always had to be aware of the neighbors, especially now that we had a young child. We had to be very mindful when she cried. After living there for about two years, we decided it was time to find a new place, somewhere that we could call home.

By selling most of my gold jewellery and using up my husband's savings, we managed to afford the down payment on our first cozy condominium. I felt as though that home belonged to us. Although it was a small one-bedroom apartment, to me it seemed like a palace. Every corner of it was a little paradise. Every tiny detail was a work of art.

Now that we had a secure home, we decided to have a second child. I was hoping to give birth to a boy this time. In our culture, the more boys you raise, the more power you have. But just one boy was fine with me. I was worried that this child would also be a girl and hoped my husband would not have a bad reaction if that were the case. The moment of truth came soon enough.

At the hospital, I lay on the bed in the examining room while the nurse checked the ultrasound.

She turned to me and smiled. "Is your first child a boy or a girl?"

"A girl," I said anxiously.

"Well luckily for you," she began. My heart jumped, waiting for her to tell me that it was a boy this time. "you do not have to buy any clothes for your second child because she can borrow her older sister's clothes." she continued cheerfully.

At that point, all I felt was disappointment.

However, after giving birth to her, my feelings completely changed as soon as I saw her face. I did not know why, but I felt a special sense of pride in her. Girl or boy, I loved her dearly from the moment she was born. My heart burst with pure happiness. I felt that one day she would be someone very special.

Then my husband entered the room carrying a basket of flowers and holding the hand of two-year-old Fatima, who was wearing a pink velvet dress. I apologized that I had not given birth to a boy. He seemed unhappy at first, but then said that it did not matter as long as she was healthy. He decided to name her Maha after his mother.

Now that I had two young children to look after, I

was busier and happier. With friends like family, a community like a garden, and a neighborhood graced by majestic scenery and parks on every corner, I no longer felt homesick. On sunny weekends, my family and I often picnicked in beautiful Stanley Park, sitting on a bright carpet of green grass shaded by thick trees like umbrellas. We also visited the beach, walking on its soft, golden sands, enlivened by the music of the soaring seagulls and the swell of the sea. My daughters loved building sandcastles, although sometimes the tide surged in and destroyed what they had built. My kids would be frustrated for a moment but then they would pick up their shovels and buckets and rebuild it to be even bigger than the first time.

Seeing this brought tears of happiness in my eyes. I had never dreamt that I would be living this wonderful moment. The family I had always wished for had become a reality. While my kids were building sandcastles, I was building new dreams for a wonderful life for them.

Chapter 11

A Family Tragedy

It's so much darker when a light goes out than it would have been if it had never shone.
- John Steinbeck

Since moving to Vancouver, we rarely went back to Dubai because flying there was too expensive, so we mainly stayed in touch with our families by calling them every once in a while.

One day, my mother called, informing me that my paternal grandfather, who was in his late seventies, had just passed away. He was a grumpy, selfish man and I can't say that I was heartbroken, especially since he had started looking for a new wife just three days after my beloved grandmother's death. After a month of searching, he settled for his Indian maid, who was in her mid-thirties.

Although he was a rich man who was worth over seventy-five million Dhs (over $20,000,000), I had never heard of him using his money to do good deeds or to help the needy. In fact, before he passed away, he revised his will so that all of his assets went to his two sons, my father and Uncle Khaldoon. Despite the fact that his daughter, Aunt Munira, had many children and had to depend on her invalid husband's military pension, which barely supported them, all he left her was an old abandoned house that was worth next to nothing. Her only hope was that her sons would graduate from university and find good jobs that would help support their household.

Meanwhile, my second brother, Rasheed, graduated with a diploma in business and my father gave him a job as his tower manager. After finding a beautiful wife for him, my mother called to say that she was planning an elaborate engagement party at a five-star hotel, and wanted me to be a part of it. I tried to explain that it was inconvenient for me to travel all the way from Canada to Dubai for a one-night celebration, especially now that I had two toddlers, but she insisted that everyone had to attend her son's first engagement party and extend their blessings for his new life. This obviously meant a lot to my mother and brother and so, after convincing my husband to let us go, my daughters and I travelled to Dubai.

As soon as I arrived, I contacted Malaka, my sister-in-law, to let her know that we were in Dubai. I had become very fond of this cheerful woman who was so full of compassion. Whenever anyone asked her for help, she would do so without hesitation. Malaka was the elder sister I had never had. When I was down, she inspired me. When I was lonely, she gave me the love that I had never received from my mother. I always thanked God for bringing her into my life.

Excited that we were in town, she was anxious to see her two young nieces, especially Maha, and wanted to come visit us.

But no matter how much I tried to persuade my mother to allow her to come, all she would say was, "No, I don't like that woman. She promised us a large sum of money, yet she did not bring us anything close. That was not acceptable."

I knew that she was just making excuses. My mother disliked anyone who was associated with me. So I decided to visit Malaka myself. I called her in the morning to tell her, but did not get an answer. I called her several times that day but did not hear back from her.

My parents' home was filled with laughter, music, and beautiful decorations, but I couldn't feel any pleasure. My intuition was telling me to prepare for some bad news, but I didn't want to accept that. I tried to convince myself that I was anxious because I was away from my husband.

That night I could not sleep. Time seemed to move in slow motion and I thought that the sun would never rise.

At around 5:00 that morning, I heard the sound of the mosque prayers. A few minutes later, I heard the phone ringing and ran to it as though I had been waiting all night for a call. My heart already heavy, I heard one of my sisters-in-law tell me some terrible news.

After midnight last night, while driving from Abu Dhabi to Dubai, Malaka, her son, and her daughter had gotten into a serious accident. Exhausted after a long day, her son, who had been driving, crashed the car into a big truck. Unfortunately, their car exploded. According to eyewitness accounts, her daughter was scratching at the window of the burning car, begging for help.

However, rescuers couldn't get there in time. Three members of our dear family all burned to death, all young. My sister-in-law was only in her early forties. My eyes dissolved into tears and I felt too weak to stand up. I heard nothing except a ticking sound. Tick, tick, tick. I did not know if the ticking was from the clock or from my heart.

After I told my husband what happened, he made immediate plans to come to Dubai for his sister's funeral. Full of sorrow, his heart ached for her. She was a kind sister, a caring mother, and his dearest friend. Now that joyful connection was gone forever. No one could fill her place in his heart. She had died and neither of us had had a chance to say good-bye. My dreams to show her my children shriveled in my heart. After the seventh day and final funeral ceremony, we were ready to travel back to Canada.

When I went to see my family to say good-bye, my mother said, "Are you crazy?! Rasheed's engagement party is in two days. You would be foolish to come all this way and then miss it!"

Usually when someone dies, to show respect for the bereaved family, there were no parties for 40 days, but my mother did not care about that in the slightest.

"She has died and that's the end of her. I have already arranged the party and I do not want to ruin it just for someone who is not even alive."

I was very angry. I told her to do whatever she wanted but not to expect me to attend the wedding.

Later on, I heard that she had thrown a lavish engagement party, soon followed by her son's extravagant three-day wedding. She even tossed gold coins to the new couple and all their guests, who excitedly collected them from the ground. After the wedding, Rasheed and his new bride set off on a splendid honeymoon to glamorous cities across the world, all expenses paid by my father. Upon their return home, my mother presented them with the biggest and most luxurious apartment in my father's high-rise, and each of them got an expensive car with which to roam the city with pride.

Meanwhile, our peaceful days in Canada passed quickly. After six years, my husband earned his PhD and it was time to return to the United Arab Emirates so that he could begin his job there. I felt sad to leave my small paradise apartment and my beautiful city with its friendly people.

During my time in Vancouver, I had learned how to fill my life with more health, joy, strength and purpose. Most importantly, I had found my key to help open the door of happiness – my husband and my daughters. It was time to say good-bye to one chapter and to prepare for a new chapter in my life.

CHAPTER 12

Happy Days on the Oasis

Generally speaking, the most miserable people I know are those who are obsessed with themselves; the happiest people I know are those who lose themselves in the service of others.
— Gordon B. Hinckley

As the first ray of sunlight danced across the horizon, the birds sang their song to the beautiful morning while the rooster awakened us with its cheerful call. This was the concert that woke me up every day.

It was the early 2000s and I was in Al Ain, a small quiet city in the oasis, 130 km from Dubai. Al Ain is famous for its legendary mountains, Jabal Hafeet, and well known for the United Arab Emirates University. I was so proud that my husband had earned a position as a university professor there. It was a badge of honor on my heart.

All of the houses and yards in Al Ain were large. Our rented six-bedroom villa, paid for by the university, was surrounded by palm trees, or *nakheels*, rising from the desert sands. Soon our lives settled into a comfortable routine. Every morning, my husband went to work and I took our eldest daughter, Fatima, to school. Afterwards, I cleaned the house, looked after Maha, cooked a meal for my family, and fed our chickens. As the clear night sky set in, I watered the *nakheels* for an hour and a half and enjoyed every second of it. The fresh, cool evening breeze carried the fragrance of the moist desert sands, which opened up my senses and cleared my mind. My bare feet would sink into the smooth, cool desert sand and I would gaze at the shining stars twinkling brightly in the sky. Meanwhile the glowing moon watched over us as the shadow of the *nakheels* fell across the golden ground.

Sometimes I felt as though I was living a life that was not my own. Blessed with everything anyone could dream of, I was filled with the happiness I had always wished for. I had to give back and so I cooked meals for the poor, donated to the needy, and helped others as much as I could. And yet something was missing.

I had a dream that I had always kept close to my heart – to open an orphanage. I knew what it was like to be an unwanted child and I remembered my cousin Abdullah, who from the time he was eight years old was constantly getting teased by the neighborhood kids for being an orphan.

"Your mom died. Your dad died. You have nobody!"

Fighting back his tears, Abdullah would scream at them, "That's not true! I have my mom and dad!"

But he couldn't deny the harsh reality – that he was alone in the world and being raised by relatives. Watching him throwing rocks at the jeering kids and crying in frustration, my heart went out to him.

I would make the little bullies leave and I'd tell him, "Don't worry, I will be like your big sister and I will always be there for you."

For years I did my best to keep my promise. From his routine days at school to the most memorable day of his life, I tried to be there for him. I explained to him the school lessons that he didn't understand and helped him with the projects that he couldn't complete on his own. When he didn't have enough money for his wedding, I designed and sewed sequins on his bride's wedding dress, decorated the stage, created centerpieces, and organized the entertainment. I always remained close friends with his wife.

Abdullah survived the hardships and became a successful and happy man with his own joyful family. That achievement fed my growing desire to hold the hands of other orphans and lead them through the storms of sorrow to lives of joy and accomplishment.

Meanwhile, my family and I attended many family celebrations, one after another. Ghalia, Mahmoud and Aunt Munira's sons all got married, and Sameera gave birth to her third child. My 22-year-old brother, Mayed, wanted to marry a babysitter from China whom he had met at a day care center on one of my father's properties, but my parents refused. Instead of backing down, he sneaked his passport out of my father's closet and left a note for my parents: "I have gone to Singapore to meet Petra's parents and I am going to marry her whether you accept it or not."

My mother was in shock. Having seen Rasheed's and Mahmoud's elaborate weddings and extravagant lifestyles, many young women were eager to marry Mayed. She had counted on arranging yet another stunning wedding so that she could once again boast in front of her guests, but that wasn't going to happen.

After a week, Mayed returned with Petra, who was now his wife.

With no choice but to make the best of it, my mother threw a small party and invited our close relatives so that she could introduce them to her new daughter-in-law. Upon meeting Petra, I could not believe my eyes. A thin woman of average height, pale skin, and sparse hair, she must have been at least 12 years older than Mayed. Why had two of my brothers chosen wives who were so much older than them? Suddenly the answer struck me. Perhaps they were looking for a woman to give them the motherly care that they had rarely received as children. I couldn't help but feel pity for them.

CHAPTER 13

THE MIRACLE

Miracles occur naturally as expressions of love. The real miracle is the love that inspires them. In this sense everything that comes from love is a miracle.
                                    - Maria Lloyd

I became pregnant at the end of the winter, and through ultrasound, discovered that it would be a boy this time. Our house was filled with joy and we all counted the days until we could welcome a new member of the family. That summer, we all travelled to Canada for our two-month vacation. Then, after our wonderful holiday, my husband and Fatima returned to Al Ain, while Maha and I stayed in Canada. My days were full of dreams.

Then, ten days before my delivery date, my mother called and told me that, due to my father's severe diabetic condition, he had developed *gangrene* in one of his feet. My parents had gone to several public and private hospitals in Dubai and all of the doctors gave the same advice – to save his life, his right foot would have to be amputated.

Knowing that my husband had developed a good network of physicians at the hospital where he had done his graduate work, my mother hoped that he would be able to refer my father to a good doctor in Vancouver. It was my father's only hope.

I felt a huge weight of responsibility on my shoulders. It was my first time alone in a country far from home, my English skills were insufficient to communicate and to do the paperwork for my father's complex case, I did not have the medical knowledge to understand what the professionals were saying, and I was unfamiliar with many areas of the city. I had lived in Vancouver for six years, but with two young children with me, I had been limited as to where I could go.

But what was even more worrisome was the fate of my son. What if my father's foot had to be amputated? I did not want my baby to be born at a time of grief. He would forever be cursed. It reminded me of the painful times when my mother would tell me that when I came into this world, I did not bring luck to my father's business, but when Sultan was born, wealth rained down upon our family.

For the sake of my unborn child, I was determined to do everything that I was capable of. I talked to my husband on the phone and did my best to acquire the knowledge and information that I needed. I also contacted some of his friends, whom he said would help guide me.

Two days later, my parents arrived. From the moment I saw my father, my heart went out to him. I held his hands and took him to the doctor's office, x-ray department, laboratory, and eventually to a specialist surgeon. We visited several different doctors to get their prognosis.

They all gave the same answer. The likelihood of saving my father's foot was extremely low and they had to make a decision quickly. Otherwise, *sepsis*, a whole-body inflammation triggered by the infection, would kill him.

I have never forgotten the day when my father was lying on the hospital bed, shivering in fear, with me and my five-year-old daughter, Maha, by his side. He started crying in anguish. With watery eyes and a shaky voice, he began to speak.

"I remember when I was 12 years old and my father took me out of school. He ordered me to start working to bring income to the house. I had to face the harsh reality of life. I worked for hours here and there doing this and that. All we have now is from my hard work. I always thought of making money. But I never thought of how to spend it. Now I regret this. I was very stupid. I wasted my whole life collecting pieces of paper."

I couldn't believe what I was hearing but he continued, "If God gives me just one more life, I would transform myself into a completely different person. I would help the needy and build a hospital, now that I know how the sick people feel. I will not only improve my life, but also the lives of many others. I will share my fortune with the unfortunate. I will give my sister Munira her rightful inheritance from my father. And I promise you that if God gives me just one more life, I will buy you an apartment in Canada."

In the 30 years that I'd known him, this was the first time that I had ever felt close to my father. I knew that his words were coming directly from his heart.

I held his hand tightly and told him, "Dear father, I know that you have good will. And I know that God will give you a chance to fulfill your promises."

"I hope so." That was all that he could say.

Then I turned around and spotted Maha, curled up, sound asleep on the blue hospital chair. I looked over at the clock on the wall. It was nearly midnight. I wished my father a good night and told him that I would visit him tomorrow. As I left the room, I felt sadness and sympathy toward him. I knew that it would take a miracle to save him. I thought about the truth that I had never known, the truth that had been hiding in my father's childhood. Behind all that roughness and anger was an insecure man.

The next morning when I was about to go and visit him, I started having contractions and had to rush myself to the hospital by taxi. When I got there, the nurse told me that I would be giving birth within a few hours. Every time I had a contraction, I prayed to God to save my father's foot. In our culture, we have a belief that if a woman prays while giving birth, her prayers will be answered. That evening, our healthy baby boy was born. We called him Mohamed.

The next day, I left the hospital. After a few days, I got a call from my mother.

She seemed very anxious as she said, "Come to the hospital as soon as possible! The doctor told us something about your father, but I'm not sure what he said."

Holding Maha's hand and carrying my newborn baby in his car seat, I quickly rushed to the hospital. I hurried through the hospital's corridors to get to my father's room, my heart pounding faster and faster. I was not sure if I was ready to say a last good-bye to him.

Finally entering his room, all that was left was an empty bed. That must mean that he had died already.

My eyes slowly filling with tears, I asked the nurse where my father was.

She noticed how upset I was and told me, "He's fine. They just took him to another room. You should talk to the doctor."

What the doctor told me was incredible. He said that what had happened to my father was a complete medical miracle. His foot was responding well to treatment. I was overcome with gratitude that God had answered my prayers.

After a few weeks, my father was released from hospital and we all went back to the United Arab Emirates. I felt happy and accomplished. Not only had I given birth to a wonderful baby boy, but also I had been able to do something else that none of my brothers could have done. I had saved our father. It was the first time in my life that my family treated me kindly. They all complimented me and they all called from time to time and asked how I was doing. They had never done that before. I enjoyed every minute of it, hoping that it would last forever.

CHAPTER 14

THE MAN OF GOD

Religion is the idol of the mob; it adores everything it does not understand.
- Frederick II

It was 2003 and now that God had spared his life, my father became a better person. Every day during *Ramadan*, he would ask his cook to prepare food for the mosque. He also kept his kitchen doors open in the afternoon, so that poor people could come in and receive a rice and chicken dish for *Iftar*. A long line of people extended from the kitchen door all the way to the street. He also bought huge supplies of rice, salt, sugar, flour, canned beans and vegetable oil, and would send his driver and an expert on poor living areas to distribute the food to the needy families. The intent was to give these families a secure basic food supply for at least two months.

My father regularly prayed in the mosque, always making sure that he stood in the first row behind the leader, the *Imam*. In fact, he prayed in *sujood*, or prostration, so much that he developed a dark mark on his forehead. To many Muslims, this mark indicated his devout faith in God and signified a pure, honest and trustworthy person.

In addition, my father provided Ali, one of Aunt Munira's sons, with a job in his office. He gave my younger sister, Ghalia, a monthly allowance of 5000

Dhs (about $1400) to support her young family. As a measure of his devotion, he also bought a beautiful apartment with a jaw-dropping view of the *Kaaba* in the holy city of Mecca. Every once in a while, he would go there to worship God.

I will never forget the times when my parents returned from Mecca. People raced to the airport to greet them, shoving one another in order to shake my parents' "good deed" hands, believing that some of their blessings would rub off on them. They called my father "Haj Hamad," a name reserved for the few people who kept God very close to their hearts. They called my mother an equally deferential name, "Hajia Fatana."

When they arrived home, cheers, tributes and a feast for family and relatives would await them. My father would go to his room and get a gallon-jug of holy water from *Zamzam*, a sacred well located within the *Masjid al-Haram* in Mecca. He would then pour the water into plastic water bottles, and distribute them to those gathered.

"I brought this from the house of God himself," he would say. "I went through the holy journey and said many prayers to bring peace to your troubles. This water will evaporate your problems. It holds a priceless value like no other gift."

People would hold their plastic bottles with gratitude, as though it were something they had been searching for their whole lives. Some of my great aunts would burst into tears of happiness, believing that my father was their key to a better life and afterlife.

Whenever people had questions about a religious topic, they would ask my father, believing that he had the knowledge of an *Imam*. Whenever they had a problem, they would tell my father about it. They considered him to be the cure for whatever ailed them. His words were the blessings of an angel. His souvenirs were holy talismans. And his name was revered throughout the family.

While my father distributed *Zamzam* water, my mother would lead my sisters-in-law to her room where they would gasp in delight as she unzipped her bags and took out sequined gowns, purses, perfumes, make-up, and much more. Later, they would all leave with gifts in their hands and smiles on their faces.

My father also opened the gates of his country estate and invited relatives and friends to come, to have fun, and to enjoy Nature's beauty. There were over four hundred palm trees on his property, as well as lemon trees, guava trees and several varieties of plants. There were also many animals, including ponies, horses, cows, chickens, goats, deer, sheep and peacocks.

My father built a huge pastel-green mansion, with 20-foot ceilings, 12 master bedrooms and four big living rooms, including a special one for VIP guests. It also had an enormous kitchen and a large dining room that could seat 48 people. In addition, there was a big indoor swimming pool and a shallow children's pool. The huge, indoor ball-pit playground was a children's paradise. In addition, in a separate outdoor building, he built four two-bedroom suites for guests.

Family and friends would gather in an outdoor sitting room with a palm straw roof and gaslights hanging from its ceiling. It was furnished in bright red patterned Arabic seating and was surrounded by beautiful ponds and fountains. People would zoom around on motorcycles, riding on special motorbike paths or setting out into the open desert close by.

It was a wonderful place to spend time with friends and family, chatting and enjoying a lavish buffet while the kids played in the outdoor playground. My family and I counted the days until the weekend when we too could participate in this amazing experience.

Chapter 15

A MIXED BLESSING

Life is a mixed blessing which we vainly try to unmix.
- Mignon McLaughlin

One afternoon, my husband had a meeting in Dubai and decided to stop by my parents' house afterwards to say hello. My father was sitting on the sofa looking so worried that he asked if there was anything bothering him. My father sighed and said that, since yesterday, the vision in his right eye was blurry and in fact his sight was almost gone. He hoped that everything would go well after a good rest, but my husband urged him to see an ophthalmologist.

After a thorough check-up, the doctor told them that my father's diabetic condition had caused severe *retinal detachment* and that if he did not have corrective surgery as soon as possible, he would be permanently blind in that eye. Unfortunately, the doctor did not know of an appropriate specialist in Dubai and suggested that my father go abroad for treatment.

My husband assured him that he would arrange an appointment for him with a specialist in Vancouver and insisted on booking a flight for that very night. The hours crept by until midnight when my parents and Sultan flew to Vancouver. Within two days, my father received eye surgery, which was declared a success.

Ten days later, he returned home with a sparkle in his eye and a smile on his face. Once more, he could see the colors of the world and the beauty of life. Once again, God had blessed him with another chance.

Grateful to my husband, he would often say, "I have always thought of you and loved you as I would love my own son."

One spring evening a few months later, I visited my parents' house and found them sitting in the living room watching a drama series on television. While sitting next to my father, I noticed that his face was pale and his breathing was loud, as though he was trying desperately to force air in and out through his nose. I asked him if he was sick and he admitted to not being able to breathe easily. After a rough night, he went to the doctor, who told him that he had an allergy and gave him a prescription.

My mother interrupted and said, "This is normal. He will just take the medicine and he will be fine." She said that this happened to many of our relatives at this time of year and was therefore not a concern. I said that this seemed more serious than an allergy and suggested that we get my husband's opinion.

"No, no. Nothing is wrong. He will be fine," my mother insisted.

But I told my father not to take chances with his health and suggested that he come with us to Canada when we went there for our summer holiday. That would give him a chance to get an expert's opinion.

My parents were delighted to accept my suggestion and came with us to Canada. My husband immediately took my father to a cardiologist, who told him that his heart condition was very worrisome. He recommended that my father undergo *angioplasty*, a special procedure that involves widening a narrowed or obstructed blood vessel. Happily, the procedure was a success. My father was so pleased that he wanted to fulfill his promise to buy me an apartment in Canada. I was thrilled. It would be the first time in my life that I had owned a property in my name.

My mother tried to put a stop to this plan. "You already have a one-bedroom apartment here. You do not need any more. Besides, you just come here for the summer vacations."

But my father did not listen to a single word she said. He went ahead and bought me a two-bedroom townhouse near the building where they had their vacation apartment. Although I was very grateful to my father, I also realized that I had just opened the window to the stinging wind of my mother's jealousy.

When we returned to Dubai, my mother told almost every single person she knew that they had bought me a townhouse in Canada. Wherever I went, I was labeled as the girl whose parents had bought her a townhouse. Because it was the first time in the history of our family that a daughter had been given such a gift, it was a very big deal. To say that this gift was a mixed blessing was an understatement.

CHAPTER 16

MONEY POURING FROM THE HEAVENS

There is no fire like passion, there is no shark like hatred, there is no snare like folly, there is no torrent like greed.
- Gautama Siddhartha

My father's fortunes continued to soar, thanks in part to Dubai's residential real estate boom. In May of 2002, expatriates were allowed to buy property in Dubai on freehold ownership, which was a first in the Middle East. In addition, investors and buyers were able to obtain resident visas for themselves and their families. Real estate developers seized the opportunity to build and sell to expatriates. Many paid a mere five to ten percent for the land and would then advertise and market their properties prior to their being built. The development costs would then fall to the buyers and investors.

Starting in 2004, my father took advantage of this situation by offering thousands of condos and office spaces for presale in seven tall towers, two of which were named after prominent Canadian cities. He also offered one thousand villas for presale. He made sure to get maximum publicity for these projects with television spots as well as large advertisements in local and international newspapers and magazines. He also took part in various national and international real estate exhibitions. My father's prices were extremely competitive, and I pointed out that he would make a lot more profit if he at least sold these properties at their market value.

But he said, "I mostly care that my customers have their dream homes at an affordable cost."

I was proud of my father – he seemed to have a genuine desire to be of service to others.

He bought a 38-story landmark building on Sheikh Zayed Street. It was already rented out to well-recognized companies and was therefore a good location for his sales and marketing offices. On both sides of the front entrance he placed two stages, each covered with bright red carpet on which stood a shiny brand new car under a spotlight. Whoever purchased more than one apartment from him would get one of the cars.

There was no shortage of journalists who, for a small kickback, would cover such stories as part of their news of the day. For example, a piece in one of the local newspapers read: "Combine one of the UAE's most dynamic and innovative property brands with one of the world's most exciting car brands, and you have the ingredients for one of the greatest promotions ever seen in the residential property market."

Because of my father's reputation as a highly devout businessman, thousands of local people were eager to buy one of his properties. Middle and lower-income investors, many of whom were from Britain, India and Iran, also rushed to buy apartments from him. Some of these expatriates purchased condos or townhouses to live in, but the majority purchased them for investment purposes.

At the peak of the market in 2005, I would see people

waiting in line outside my father's new sales office. It was as if they were trying to get into a popular movie or theatre production. I was surprised when my friend Farima told me that her father had used his store as collateral to borrow a huge sum of money from the bank in order to buy one of my father's condos.

Money was raining down from the heavens onto my family. They had so much money that spending it became a full-time occupation. My father bought a beautiful piece of land in Jumeirah, a prestigious neighborhood favored by celebrities and by the affluent. With its stunning view of the beach, it was the perfect place to build his dream home.

He also bought vacation apartments in Canada, England, Malaysia, Singapore and other locations worldwide. Having international real estate holdings meant that he opened up a number of bank accounts abroad. In addition, he purchased a private yacht and bought several VIP license plates for himself, my mother, my brothers, and their wives. Sometimes the plates cost more than the cars.

Not content to merely own the latest Rolls Royce, Lamborghini, Ferrari, and/or Mercedes-Benz, my brothers also collected over one hundred classic cars. They all had high salaries and their own Jumeirah villas and spent their summer vacations in London, Paris, Switzerland, Italy, Australia, Canada, Singapore and many other places around the world. They had private drivers, housekeepers and private chefs. Their children not only attended expensive private schools but each had his or her own babysitter.

Not having to care for their homes, their husbands,

or their children, my brothers' wives could indulge in a decadent lifestyle, casually wearing their diamonds in public, stirring up the envy of others. After they got tired of shopping for brand-name clothing, handbags, shoes and accessories, my sisters-in-law would relax at a fancy spa or enjoy an elaborate meal at a fine-dining restaurant at a glamorous five-star hotel.

When one of her daughters-in-law became pregnant, my mother would reserve the hospital's VIP suite, outfitted with high-end décor and designer bedding, so that the mother-to-be could deliver her baby in style and visitors could be treated to fancy hors d'oeuvres and expensive gifts.

I couldn't help feeling envious of this luxurious lifestyle and at one point pleaded with my father to share his largesse with me, as he'd done with my brothers. I reminded him that I had worked hard since I was a child, cleaning the house and babysitting his other children. Irritated, he reminded me that he had already bought me a townhouse. That was more than enough for me.

"And also, if you haven't noticed, your brothers actually work for me."

I told him that I could work for him as well. I may not have much experience but I had a good education, I had the knowledge to make his business prosper and, having lived in Canada for years, I had seen how successful managers treated their employees and customers. I pleaded with him to give me a chance. But all he said was that I could get myself a job if I wanted to, but not in his business.

"I don't want your work and we never give positions to girls, so forget it."

Hearing this, my mother narrowed her eyes and smiled contemptuously as she told me that I was greedy for money and envious of my brothers, reminding me that my brothers carried the family name. When they dressed well, it reflected well on our family. When they lived in style, our family looked prosperous. But since my children did not carry the family name, I would never carry the family's wealth.

After reminding me of having told me that once I got married I would be on my own, she stuck the knife in further when she said, "We have a saying here. Do not look up too high or your neck will break."

All I could feel was deep sadness. My sister, Ghalia, and I saw all of the other members of my family enjoying a life of luxury. We felt discriminated against and it hurt. But although their insults and disrespectful comments were painful, losing my parents would have been even more painful. In the public eye, we were highly regarded as members of a wealthy family. Associated with them, I had a place in society. But such prestige was also a source of frustration and irritation because whenever I bought something for myself, others would wrongly assume that it was a gift from my father.

My parents had always discriminated against me, but in the past I had never considered it to be unusual. However, having spent a number of years in Canada, I met many parents who loved and treated all of their children equally. They did not care whether their child was a boy or a girl.

CHAPTER 17

DARK SECRETS

Three things cannot be long hidden: the sun, the moon, and the truth.
—Gautama Siddhartha

One afternoon, while approaching my parents' house, I noticed an anxious-looking woman standing next to the drop-off place by the garage where they placed the food for the poor. I greeted her and soon found out that she was the expert on poor living areas whom my parents had hired. I invited her inside and said that I would let my mother know that she was here. She hastily declined, saying that my mother was not yet home and that she would wait outside until she arrived.

"God bless you," I said to her, "You are doing a great job helping the needy. It can't be easy."

Her reply shocked me. "Actually, I am here to tell your parents that I will not continue this work any longer."

She went on to explain that, although my parents provided a lot of food, it was not of much use. Most of it was expired or close to it, and much of it was of very poor quality. Many of the poor people had complained to her that the food had made them sick. She and the others responsible for distributing the food to the poor would prefer that my parents gave them money instead.

That would be better for the poor people and easier for my parents.

I couldn't believe what I was hearing. Why would my parents buy expired or low-quality items when they were blessed with more money than they knew what to do with? Even high-quality food would be a bargain for them.

It was at that moment that I saw a large, brand-new, black Mercedes-Benz SUV driving through my parents' gates. The car doors opened and my mother and sisters-in-law emerged, all giggling and carrying shopping bags. My eyes were drawn to a huge ruby ring on my mother's finger and an enormous gold watch surrounded by diamonds on her wrist. When she caught sight of the woman standing next to me, the expression on her face instantly changed from gleeful to annoyed. She approached us and told me to go inside.

Watching the ensuing conversation through the French doors, I saw my mother throwing up her arms, shaking her head, and arguing with every suggestion that the poor woman tried to make.

Meanwhile, my sisters-in-law were trying on their new diamond necklaces and admiring themselves in the mirror. Rasheed's wife told me that they'd been to a jewellery exhibition.

"Your mother is very generous. She told us that since we were her daughter-in-laws, we should only wear the best of the best. So she allowed us to buy whatever we desired."

I smiled but I was aching inside, wishing that my mother would treat me with such generosity. But I tried to convince myself that I did not need those jewels. I could live without them.

After about ten minutes, my mother rushed in angrily and announced to all of us: "That lady is very hungry for money. She wants us to buy the food from a store that she recommends. But I know she just wants to get a commission. She told us the other option was to give her cash to distribute it to the poor. She just wants to steal all the money for herself. She is turning into a thief. We have to find a new person to replace her."

I listened in confusion. Who was I to believe?

Then one day I visited Aunt Munira and, when I stepped through her gate, I couldn't help noticing that her house was getting very decrepit. The outside walls, formerly white, were marred by long cracks filled with green fungus. When I set foot inside, her grey carpets looked shabby and worn and the sofa was very dirty. Even its dark maroon color could not camouflage its many stains. Finding my aunt in the living room, she seemed worried. Although she was only in her fifties, her face was a mass of wrinkles. Despite her unhappy state, she offered me tea.

I asked her why she was so upset. She sighed and explained that her third son, who wanted to get married, had graduated and had a job, but his salary was insufficient for the new couple to have their own home, which meant that they would have to live with her. However, her tiny house didn't have enough space for them, especially now that her first and second sons and their families were already living there. She wanted to transform her garage into a separate suite, but the heavy price tag held her back.

Confused, I said to her, "Hadn't my father given Ali a job with a good salary?"

She shook her head sadly and explained that when Ali worked for the Dubai Electric and Water Authority, he had a secure job and peace of mind. But then my father and brothers told him that he was wasting his time and would make a lot more money if he worked for them. They promised him a much better salary as well as a commission.

She remembered him telling her, "Mother, we can build a bigger house, eat better food, buy a better car and live a better life. I will have enough money for you to enjoy your life."

My aunt had never seen him that happy. He was inspired to work long hours, always telling her that this would be the end of their miserable life. Sadly, it was just the beginning.

Seeing my bewilderment, she explained that the salary that Ali received from my father's company was very low and sometimes they "forgot" to pay him. He worked day and night because he had been promised that if he brought in a lot of customers, he would get a handsome sales commission and an increase in salary. Although Ali succeeded in bringing in many investors, he was told that they would pay his commission and increase his salary "next time." Days turned into weeks and weeks turned into months, but "next time" became "never." When he asked for his money, my brothers told him that the company had changed the rules and no longer provided salary increases or commissions. It was obvious that my father had only hired Ali for his own self-interest.

Shedding more light on the situation, Aunt Munira told me about the government's Emiratization policy, which required that all medium to large-sized businesses hire a certain number of local employees. Wanting to distinguish himself from other developers by presenting himself as a trustworthy "native son," thereby making locals more willing to purchase real estate from him, my father used Ali as a local recruiter, making good use of Ali's ability to speak many languages, including Arabic, English, Urdu, Persian, and Russian. Having Ali on staff also increased his company's credibility with the authorities.

But once Ali had served his purpose and had brought in the buyers, my brothers began humiliating him by doing things like throwing a pencil on the ground and ordering him to fetch it like a dog, or embarrassing him in front of customers by yelling at him for no reason. They even lied to Ali's wife and said that they'd seen him with another woman. These lies made her suspicious of Ali and eroded her love and trust in him.

Just the day before, my brothers had called Ali and told him to stand outside the door and get a surprise. Driving up in their Lamborghini, one of my brothers rolled down the tinted window and handed Ali a white plastic grocery bag. With his wife standing on the porch watching, Ali opened the bag to find a bunch of chicken bones.

I was horrified by my brothers' despicable behavior and wondered if Ali could return to his old job. My aunt said that someone had already replaced him and it was very difficult to find another job.

"Why hasn't Ali complained to my father?"

Munira explained that he tried but all that happened is that my father told him that he gets a good salary and the opportunity to eat in fancy restaurants with my brothers when they have VIP guests, plus he gets to visit the country estate on the weekend with his wife. Ali had never had these opportunities before and he should be very grateful.

I tried another tack. Now that my father and Uncle Khaldoon were making lots of money, couldn't she request her share of their father's inheritance?

But she explained that a few days before his death, her father wrote that all of his assets would go to her brothers and said, "We do not let our assets go outside our family," as though women were not a part of the family. This was a longstanding rule that had been passed along from generation to generation. Whenever my aunt asked her brothers, their response was always the same.

"You will have nothing. We would never ever give anything to the girls in our family."

She was powerless to do anything about it.

"Why don't you stand up for your rights and take them to court?"

She told me that was easier said than done. First of all, her husband was sick and therefore he wouldn't be able to stand by her and help her face the legal challenges. Second, she needed a good lawyer but didn't have the money to pay for one. Finally, even if she did take her brothers to court, the community would look upon her as a bad person who destroyed her family because of her envy and greed.

Determined to help, I assured her that I would talk to my father right away and sort things out. She tried to discourage me, saying that, as far as her inheritance was concerned, she already knew his answer. Instead, she was planning to sell her wedding jewellery, much as it pained her to do so. She had to have money to do the renovation. Her plan was to rent out the new suite and hopefully make some money to help her children.

I knew that she was right about her inheritance, but my brothers were to blame for Ali's job situation. I reasoned that my father was probably unaware of what was going on and there was no harm in letting him know. But that evening, when I arrived at my father's shopping mall, I was horrified to see two brutish Nigerian bodyguards grabbing a Filipino man, whom I recognized as one of my father's employees, and pulling him toward a waiting taxicab.

The employee was dragging his heels and crying helplessly, pleading with them to stop. However, the bodyguards roughly shoved him in the cab, locked the door and drove away with him. The Filipino man looked directly at me through the back window, as though asking for my help. The mall was crowded and there was no shortage of witnesses silently watching the incident, but everyone was too afraid to interfere.

Trying to get to the bottom of what had just happened, I approached one of the mall's security guards standing by the front entrance. He looked very upset, having watched the whole scene. He explained to me that my father had just learned about a new law imposed by the Ministry of Labour requiring employers to pay their employees an end-of-service benefit (EOSB) or gratuity. As a result, he had ordered his employees to sign an agreement waiving their right to receive it. The Filipino gentleman had refused to sign and my father wanted to teach him a lesson – he would be blacklisted and deported from the country, never to return again.

I was so distressed to hear this. Despite the mounting evidence to the contrary, I held out hope that my father was the changed man that he had appeared to be in the hospital room in Vancouver. I had seen him treat his maids and other employees with disrespect, but could he really be so unjust as to prevent poor people from receiving what was rightfully theirs?

I knew that he would be angry if I were to visit him at his workplace, but my desire to help my aunt was stronger than my fear of him. It was a long elevator ride up to his office. When I arrived, the secretary asked if I wanted her to inform him that I was there.

"It's alright," I said. "Don't bother him. I can wait."

I waited in the secretary's office for 30 painful minutes, during which I saw a long line of frightened employees entering my father's office one at a time to sign the agreement, and then exiting with their heads down. Some of them even burst into tears. My heart went out to them but to give my father the benefit of the doubt, I thought that perhaps he was unaware that such actions would harm him in the end. If he took away his employees' rights, they would lose their faith in him. If he treated them with injustice, they would see him as a tyrant. I may not have known much about managing employees, but I knew that much.

After the last employee had signed the agreement, I entered my father's office. The room was dark, illuminated only by a dimly lit lamp in the corner. The curtains were closed without a streak of sunlight entering the room. To intensify the feeling of gloom, the walls, sofa, leather office chair, glass desk, curtains and carpet were all dark green. On the walls were dozens of framed pictures of his towers, each placed in its own black frame like a trophy.

The moment my father saw me, he visibly tensed up, and he screamed at me, "What the hell are you doing here!?!"

I had intended to tell him the consequences of his harsh actions toward his poor employees but, seeing his enraged face, I immediately froze with fear, overcome by terrifying memories of the brutal beatings that I had received as a child. All I could say was that I had come to ask how he was doing. He replied that he knew how to take care of himself and no longer needed my help or advice. I started to say that I had seen Aunt Munira that afternoon and had found out that her son wanted to get married, but he interrupted me before I could finish my sentence and said that no matter how much money he gave her, my aunt would never be satisfied. She was always greedy for more. He said that he had already given her son a good job.

Before I could say anything further, he got up and said that he had to go to the mosque for the evening prayers and that I was welcome to come to dinner at their place before returning to Al Ain.

Before leaving, he turned and said pointedly, "Do not EVER come to my office again, do you understand?"

CHAPTER 18

THE END OF SAMEERA

The search for a scapegoat is the easiest of all hunting expeditions.
- Dwight D. Eisenhower

I left my father's office in despair and took the elevator down to the main floor. There in the nearby coffee shop, I saw Sultan, now 30, sitting cozily and laughing flirtatiously with a Filipino woman who appeared to be in her early forties.

She was short with dark skin, narrow eyes and thick, black hair. She looked familiar, and then I remembered that she owned a tailor shop in the mall. I wanted to turn a blind eye and not let them know that I'd seen them, but they saw me and I was forced to approach them.

Introducing me to his companion, Sultan said, "This is Margie, she is my fiancée."

After mumbling a polite response, I said goodbye and left. I felt pity for Sameera, his wife and the mother of his three children. She would not be pleased and neither would my mother, I thought.

That evening, I visited our parents' home to have dinner and to check on Sameera. My mother was drinking tea, cracking sunflower seeds and watching television. I greeted her and asked where Sameera was. She told me that she was in her room.

"Why do you want to see her?"

I was hesitant to tell her about Sultan's new fiancée, but after doing so, I found out that not only had my mother already met her but she also thought that Margie was a smart woman and a much better wife for Sultan than Sameera. Unlike Sameera, she was a business owner and definitely knew how to make money. This time, she didn't seem to care about her son's fiancée's age or culture. She then paused and asked me anxiously how I knew about Margie. I said that I had seen her with Sultan after visiting my father at his office.

"Why did you go there!?!"

I explained that I had just wanted to tell him about Aunt Munira's situation.

"Mind your own business! Stop sticking your nose into other people's lives."

After leaving my mother, I nervously approached Sameera's room and knocked on her door. When she didn't answer, I kept knocking and calling her name until she eventually unlocked it. Her room was dark, the bed was unmade, and clothes were scattered everywhere. Her eyes were red and she had obviously been crying. Not wanting to reveal that I knew about Margie, I asked what was the matter. Her voice trembling, she said that her days with our family were coming to an end. Sultan wanted to marry another woman and my parents had agreed. They wanted to get rid of her and take away her children.

"As their mother, you have a right to your children," I reminded her, "And besides, why would my parents take them away from you?"

She explained that they would not let her live with her children because they did not want to have to pay for her shelter or for her children's monthly allowance as the law required. From her point of view, my mother saw the kids as her toys, as a way for her to feel young again. Sameera said that my mother was taking away her happiness for her own ends. I knew that she was right and there was nothing I could do about it.

At dinner, my father seemed to have cooled off toward me and he started telling us about his day at the office.

"First they come begging for a job. And after I give them the job, day after day they demand more and more. They think I grow money on trees!"

I didn't share this perspective but I was too afraid to oppose him.

The next weekend, I decided to check on Sameera again. There was no one in the living room except for Sameera's kids, who were playing peacefully on the carpet. When I knocked on her bedroom door, no one answered. I tried the doorknob and it was unlocked. When I entered her room, I saw her lying on the floor, groaning quietly. I was horrified to see a bottle of pills in her hand. I yelled for our maid to come and help. We picked up Sameera, placed her in my car, and rushed to Emergency. Upon hearing what had happened, the attending doctor started treating her immediately. I waited in the hallway, thinking of her lying helplessly and motionlessly on the hospital bed.

There lay a woman whose life had become a living hell. When she married Sultan, she was full of hopes and dreams and thought that the gateways of heaven had opened for her. She had no way of knowing that her hopes would fade away and her dreams would become her worst nightmares. My family had made her life so miserable that she could not take it anymore.

In about two hours, a doctor finally came and said that she was out of danger but she needed to stay overnight so they could make sure that she was stable. I called and told my parents about Sameera, not anticipating that they would take advantage of her suffering. But they did. They obtained a copy of the hospital report stating that Sameera had mental health problems and was therefore unfit to take care of her young children. When the case went to court, the judge declared that Sameera no longer had the right to raise her children and that my parents and Sultan would be responsible for their care. Sameera could visit her kids twice a week for a couple of hours. Case closed. Sultan and my parents got exactly what they wanted. He soon divorced her, leaving her with very little money.

Over time, my mother filled Sameera's children's ears with ugly lies about their mother.

"She does not love you. She got rid of you. She left you and your father to marry another man. If she brings you any candies, don't eat them because she put poison inside them to kill you. If she gives you any toys, don't take them because she does not love you. She only loves your money."

Whenever Sameera visited their house, Hamad, eight years old, would slam the French door in her face before she set foot inside. Or he would spit in her face and pull her hair. Sometimes he would fill a jug with water and pour it on her. Three-year-old Mahmoud would sit and watch with his big brown eyes, not understanding what was happening, but wanting to copy his brother.

Sameera's daughter, Shamsa, six, would yell, "You are a bitch! We hate you. Don't come here again."

Helpless to defend herself or to reach the children whom she had already lost, Sameera would sit in one spot, without moving a single muscle or saying a single word, tears running down her face. I saw my mother standing at a distance, smiling and enjoying every second of the performance. She was her grandchildren's teacher.

However, if there were unexpected guests present, she would turn on her other face.

"No, Hamad. No, Shamsa. Don't treat her that way. She is your mother, so be nice."

I tried to convince Sameera's children to treat their mother with kindness, but they wouldn't listen to me. So I tried to bring my mother to her senses. When I asked her why she would try to separate her grandchildren from their mother, she justified her behavior by saying that Sameera was crazy and the children were better off without her. Week after week, she managed to get Sameera to come over less and less and hired a Malaysian maid to look after her children instead. Every once in a while, she would take her grandchildren out in public. Sometimes strangers would ask if they were her kids.

"Yes," she would reply with pride.

Although well into her fifties, she seemed to think that they were her key to eternal youth.

Soon afterwards, Sultan married Margie and they moved into a deluxe apartment. It was Margie's third marriage. From the moment she became part of our family, she got a senior position in my father's business (despite my father having told me that he never gave positions to girls) and immediately started giving out jobs to her relatives from the Philippines. She also persuaded my father to fire Aunt Munira's son, Ali. My father was impressed by Margie's business savvy. Like my mother, he saw her as a clever woman who knew how to make money.

Some of his employees told me that he placed two desks outside their sales department, one for Margie and the other one for Petra, my brother Mayed's wife. Buyers passing by their desks to purchase an apartment had to pay either Margie or Petra a two percent commission.

When buyers asked why they should pay this sum to them when they were buying directly from the developer, their response was, "That's the rules here. If you don't want to pay, then don't waste our time. Thousands of people are waiting for this opportunity."

Despite this nonsense, people were fighting to buy the apartments. They would even sign agreements without reading them carefully.

I assumed that the real reason behind Margie and Petra's commissions was that my father wanted to make them and my brothers rich and happy. Another reason was that he wanted to encourage them to bring in customers from China and the Philippines. Before long, my father's business had stretched across the globe. Margie and Sultan travelled to the Philippines and many other countries to open up more sales offices. Eventually, they sold thousands of apartments and villas. But at one point their visits to the Philippines suddenly stopped, even though it was Margie's home country. I would later find out why.

CHAPTER 19

THE VICTIMS' BAIT

The mother of excess is not joy but joylessness.
— Friedrich Nietzsche

On the weekends, I would wake up with the sun at our home in Al Ain and make pastries, salads, and finger foods to serve my parents and their guests. Then my family and I would hop in the car and, with delicious food on our laps, we would drive to my father's country estate. To my kids, it was an amusement park. To me, it was a family home.

But that was before I discovered that for my father it was a place to ensnare and deceive the naïve, the poor, and the greedy – if they were in some way useful to him. One of these unfortunate individuals was a police officer who was married to a Filipino lady who later told me the whole story.

One day, the police officer's wife stopped by Margie's shop to get a dress made. Soon the two of them started chatting and Margie learned about her customer's husband's profession. That gave her an idea. Margie knew that my father wanted to make a higher profit on his rentals by increasing the rents by 30 percent, but tenancy agreements only allowed for a five percent annual increase. The only way he could get the increase that he wanted was if his old tenants left and new ones came in. His first strategy was to reduce the amount of maintenance on the apartments. When his tenants complained that repairs were not being taken care of, he would tell them that if they weren't happy, they could leave. Another tactic involved looking for excuses to evict them from their homes.

Anticipating a commission, Margie suggested to my father that sending a uniformed policeman to the door would scare tenants into packing up their belongings and leaving. My father thought that was a great idea and so Margie invited the police officer and his family to spend weekends at my father's country estate. There, they would enjoy a delicious barbecue, chat with the other guests, and have a wonderful time. His kids loved it. After a few delightful weekends, my father introduced him to his plan. The police officer felt put on the spot and hesitated, uneasy about using his profession in such an unethical manner. But seeing his beloved family enjoying themselves, and not wanting to disappoint them, he decided that he would not lose anything by accepting the deal.

Day after day, the policeman, along with my brothers, would bang on some of the tenants' doors. Without offering any explanation, he told them that they had a week to pack and leave the apartment. Easily petrified by a man in uniform, these Filipino and Indian tenants left their homes in fear. The police officer did a good job, but once he had helped my family get rid of the unwanted tenants, they did not need him anymore, and so they got rid of him.

They did this by no longer greeting him and his family with friendly faces, but instead treating them as unwanted guests, doing everything they could to make them feel uncomfortable and unwelcome. Margie deliberately provoked a fight with the officer's wife. Soon, the police officer and his family no longer visited the country estate. They were not the only people who were used up and then disposed of in this way.

In order to obtain extra loans with great financial terms, my father would invite bank managers and their families to spend weekends at the estate as well. He was obsessed with bank loans, considering them to be "free money," and would go to great lengths to maximize the loans for his business dealings.

Overhearing conversations among my brothers and father, I came to understand that my father offered the same buildings as collateral to multiple banks in order to get loans from several sources. On other occasions, he would use correspondence from rival banks as leverage to get loans from another bank at preferred interest rates.

My brothers had a scam that involved altering the letters that my father had received from banks describing the value of the loans that they were offering. They would tamper with these letters, increase the rate and value of the loans that the banks were offering, and then send a copy of the "revised" letters to competing banks to persuade them to provide my father with the loan and interest rate that he wanted.

Another strategy for maximizing his loans involved providing the banks with phony tenancy agreements and forged documents that inflated his income from his properties. High-end scanners and printers were a great help. My brother, Mayed, was an expert in the use of scanners. I was amazed at how readily the banks fell for these sorts of tactics. Perhaps it was because there was no communication or cooperation between banks, only competition.

In another instance, my father bribed a government employee to provide him with a better deal on one of his industrial projects. The young employee became so accustomed to receiving bribes from my father that he got involved in similar schemes with different investors. Eventually, he got caught and spent a number of years in jail.

One of the most obvious of my father's stooges was a short, overweight individual who called himself "Engineer Mustafa." I first met him one weekend when we were having lunch at the estate.

My father said, "Let it be my honor to introduce you to Engineer Mustafa. I hired him from Ajman because of his great knowledge and experience in the art of architecture. He is the one who is designing and constructing our seven towers."

Although he was carrying pictures of buildings, this man seemed more like the kind of person who sat, ate, and talked for most of his life. I felt sorry for my father's buyers who paid a good amount of money for such an obviously unprofessional man. With all of the fine prospects available to him, why would my father hire him? Especially since my father had hired a well-known professional engineering firm for the construction of his private buildings.

After the man left, I asked my father, "Do you think Engineer Mustafa is qualified to construct all seven of your towers?"

In response, my father showed me pictures of seven

marvelous skyscrapers. "He is the one who designed these masterpieces."

I couldn't help feeling skeptical.

That evening, I saw three men and a woman stepping out of a big black Range Rover. They were all dressed in formal suits. The woman and one of the men were in their thirties while the other two men appeared to be in their late forties. They all spoke English with a Russian accent. The woman seemed more fluent in English than the others.

My parents welcomed them as though they were royalty, and my brothers were on their best behavior. My family led their guests to their VIP living room and shut the door. It was obvious that they did not want anyone to disturb them. Afterwards, I asked Margie who they were.

"They are consultants from overseas who have come to set up your father's new aluminum and glass companies," she replied.

Deciding to help prepare a feast for them, I went outside to assist our Indian cook who was preparing food on the barbecue. The weather was extremely hot and the large flaming grill made it even warmer. Drops of sweat ran down our cook's face. Next to him was a bucketful of delicious-looking seafood. My parents had obviously been expecting these important guests. We started placing the seafood on the grill.

A few minutes later, I saw Sultan come up and look at the grill. Then I heard a very loud slapping sound. I looked and saw that, for no apparent reason, my brother had slapped the daylights out of our cook. Although his heart must have been pounding in fear, the cook did not move a single muscle but just stared helplessly at the burning grill. It was obvious that this was not the first time that he had been beaten.

I was incredibly angry, and I yelled at Sultan, "Why did you slap him!?!"

He yelled back, "He is an animal, an animal! He has no brain! I told him to put the lobsters on the grill first." And then he left.

I felt terrible and kept apologizing to this poor man. Since I had been helping him, I felt responsible for his being so cruelly punished.

Soon my mother came to check on the food. When the cook left to get some plates, I took the opportunity to tell my mother how I felt.

"Sultan's heart is like a cold stone. He slapped our cook, as though the man does not have any feelings."

As usual, my mother stood up for her son.

"He deserved that. He has a very dirty eye looking at our female servants."

After dinner, the guests left and I had to leave as well. Before going back to Al Ain, I wanted to check on the cook and to say good-bye. I saw him hiding behind a large pile of dishes, washing them with his head down. I grabbed fifty Dhs from my purse and gave it to him.

"Buy yourself a treat, you deserve it. I am sure the special guests enjoyed the splendid seafood feast that you prepared."

"Those are not special guests. I see those Russian people in the office quite often."

Looking over to see who was talking, I discovered that it was Abdul Salam, who was sitting comfortably at the table drinking chai. Abdul Salam was the Indian cook who had worked for us since he was 20 years old. Because of his honesty and loyalty, my father had promoted him to a job in his office.

I assumed that he saw our visitors frequently because they were consulting with my father about his aluminum and glass companies. However, Abdul Salam said that he knew nothing about that but he often saw them presenting my father with a suitcase full of money. Then my father would present the Russians with a cheque and would give Abdul Salam a portion of the money to deposit as proceeds from his rental apartments. If it were a very large sum, as it often was, my father and Sultan would divide up the cash and ask Abdul Salam to deposit the money into several banks.

Proudly, he said that my father only trusted him with his valuable money. He said that he also took deposit money from Haj Vali, an Iranian businessman. Unlike the arrogant Russians, Abdul Salam said that Haj Vali was humble and down to earth.

It was the end of our conversation, but the beginning of a whole new understanding of my father. Could my father be money laundering? I knew that he was a brutish man who had lived a brutish life, and I knew that my family dearly loved money, but I never thought that they would cross the line into criminality. I felt bewildered.

But then I thought about him praying at the mosque and helping the needy. In the house of every family member there were *prayer rugs, prayer beads*, and bottles of *Zamzam* holy water, which my father had brought back from his monthly pilgrimages to Mecca. No, it could not possibly be true, I decided.

CHAPTER 20

THE EVIDENCE MOUNTS

When crimes begin to pile up they become invisible. When sufferings become unendurable, the cries are no longer heard. The cries, too, fall like rain in summer.
- Bertolt Brecht

I couldn't break my bonds of trust with my family. I needed to believe that the rumors that I was hearing about my father's business were all a misunderstanding. However, no matter how hard I tried to believe in his innocence, the evidence kept mounting and my doubts kept getting stronger.

One afternoon, it was Mayed's son's birthday party and my family had a huge celebration for him at my father's mall. It took place in the children's "fun zone" where there were clowns, magicians, shows, music, play areas, cakes, pizza, drinks, candy, gifts, colorful decorations and much more. Everyone was laughing and having a good time. My mother asked me to come to my father's office to help her carry her grandson's large surprise gift.

When we arrived, my father was drinking tea at his desk while watching a soccer match on television. As he saw my mother, his face brightened and he asked her to join him for tea but my mother told him that we had just come to get the gift and to ask him to join the party.

Suddenly, we heard a knock at the door and, after

being invited to come in, a tall, thin, grey-bearded Pakistani man in his late fifties and wearing shabby clothing entered the room. He told my father that he had finished working on the air conditioners. Because my father had promised him more job opportunities if he was satisfied, he said that he had worked very hard to make sure that the work was excellent. He also said that he had completed the job in 10 days instead of two weeks because he had hired workers from the neighboring air-conditioning shop.

"Good job, good job. So how much did I pay you as a down payment?" my father asked.

The man replied that he had paid him 30,000 Dhs and owed him another 70,000.

"Seventy thousand! I don't think I remember that deal."

My father then searched his drawers and cabinets without finding anything. I could see a sinister gleam in his eye.

"Don't worry, Boss. I have the original bill with me."

The repairman took the bill out of his pocket and handed it to my father. After carefully reading the bill, my father ripped it into tiny pieces and threw it into the trash. The man's eyes widened in shock. My father then took out some cash from his drawer and placed it on the desk. The man stared in disbelief and started counting the money as though my father was joking.

"This is only 20,000 dirhams!" he said, not able to believe what was happening. "I worked very hard for you. Why are you doing this to me? Have mercy. I need that money!" he cried.

At that point, my father yelled, "Get out!" and the

two big Nigerian bodyguards roughly grabbed him and pulled him out of the room. The man no longer had anyone to look up to and so he looked up to the sky, to God, tears running down his face.

"Those people are greedy. They know that you are rich so they want to use you. What you did was good. They don't deserve anything. Now let's go down to the party and have fun," my mother said happily.

During the party, I saw my parents laughing, eating and joking as though nothing had happened. I couldn't believe my eyes. Just half an hour ago they had shattered a poor man's hopes. Behind their enjoyment was disgraceful behavior.

In fact, because I had been too afraid to oppose them, I felt as though I too was disgraceful. In an attempt to make myself feel better, I reminded myself that even if I had tried to stop them, they wouldn't listen to me. They had everything they wanted and could do anything they wanted. They would not give that up for me or for anyone. And I couldn't tell anyone else because they wouldn't believe me. Even if they did, I was afraid that they would blame me because they would assume that, since I was their daughter, I was also their partner in crime. How could I live with that?

Chapter 21

The End of Me

Then I discovered that being related is no guarantee of love.
— Stieg Larsson

My family and I visited my parents' country estate the next weekend, as we usually did, but this time my family treated us differently.

After lunch, I tried to join my sisters-in-law in their giggly conversation, but as soon as I sat down they all grew silent, crossed their legs and arms and looked at me with cold, unfriendly expressions on their faces. When I tried to talk to them, I felt as though I was talking to myself. One by one, they all got up and left me sitting there alone.

Simple exchanges with my father turned into furious fights. He took every word I said from a negative perspective.

My mother seemed to be looking for things to complain about.

"This cake you brought today is too sweet. There is too much sugar. You know your father has diabetes. Do you want to make him sick?"

I said that I used the same recipe with the same ingredients and proportions as I had always done.

"Oh and your kids' clothes are very cheap. Why are you so stingy?"

Half an hour later, my kids ran up to me, looking unhappy. "Hamad and Shamsa won't let us play with their toys," said Maha.

"They told us to never come here again," complained Fatima.

Trying to soothe them, I said that it was time to go back home to Al Ain. Entering the kitchen to get my cake plate, I looked over at the empty chair where Abdul Salam usually sat and then asked the cook where he was. The cook lowered his head and said that Abdul Salam had been fired.

"Your father said that he stole one hundred thousand dirhams from him."

Shocked, I said that I had known Abdul Salam for a long time. He was an honest and pure person. He would never steal. I also knew that my father would not simply fire someone without recovering his money and taking legal action for any wrongdoing. Most likely he did not want his secrets to be exposed.

"Next week, I will also leave," said the cook. "They will fire me, but I am glad. I will return back to India. I am tired of working here at this stressful job. I want to see my wife and children. I miss them so much."

I told him that he was a great man and I knew that he would have a great future. I wished him and his family all happiness, health and luck in the years ahead. I could see that this lightened his heart – it didn't seem as though anyone had ever spoken to him in this way.

He looked to see if there was anyone around. Speaking softly, he said, "I will tell you something. But don't tell anyone I told you this."

I assured him that I wouldn't.

"This morning I heard your family talking in the dining room. They said that you know a lot of secrets and they do not want you to know more. So they want to get rid of you."

Walking away from the cook, I felt stunned, as though I'd been hit.

Despite my distaste for many of the things that they did and had done, I couldn't help feeling hurt that my family no longer trusted me. I had always been faithful to them. I had always hidden their ugly secrets and showcased their beauty.

In society, I was considered one of them. If they were honored, I was respected. If they fell, I would collapse. And if they were criminals, so was I. I had sacrificed a great deal of my integrity for them. Despite everything, they were at the center of my life.

With a heavy heart, I said good-bye to them all and drove back to Al Ain. I had seen this pattern with others and now it was happening to my family and me.

When my father was sick, they took advantage of my husband's knowledge. We were useful to them. But after we had helped them several times, if my father needed medical treatment, they knew how to get to Vancouver, and they knew the names and numbers of the appropriate people to contact. They knew the city well enough that they could find their way to the hospital, and they knew how to get help with the paperwork.

Now that we had nothing to offer them, we were nothing but an inconvenience.

CHAPTER 22

THE DEVIL IS IN THE FINE PRINT

To sin is a human business, to justify sins is a devilish business.
- Tolstoy

In 2008, my growing doubts about my father's innocence were confirmed when my dear friend, Farima, revealed a truth that I had long suspected. A woman in her mid-30s with a pleasant, cheerful and sincere personality, Farima was a teacher who was originally from Iran but who had lived most of her life in Dubai. For many years, her father had a clothing store in Al Karama, an old and established low-income residential and retail district. Her husband also worked in her father's store and they all lived together in a tiny two-bedroom apartment. Every penny they earned came from sweat and hard work.

One day, Farima called, obviously devastated, and reminded me of the large loan that her father had taken from the bank so that he could buy an apartment in one of my father's buildings. Enticed by all of the advertisements, he had hopes that when the building was completed, he would be able to sell it at a large profit, as had many other investors in those days. However, to their shock and disappointment, in the four years since her father had purchased the apartment, my father hadn't even started to build the tower. Instead, he had used their money and the money from many other investors to build his own private towers.

Farima's father begged him, "Please return my money. We do not have any money. I took this loan from the bank and it is putting us into a very difficult spot. This pressure and stress is crushing my family."

But my father did not feel any sympathy or guilt toward him. Instead, he said that he would only return the money if her father went to Iran and found him a beautiful 18-year-old girl so that my father could get married to her secretly. Farima's father did not know what to do. He needed the money and didn't feel as though he had any choice but to comply.

But when he went home and told them what had happened, her mother said, "Don't fear him, fear God. You would destroy his family, his wife and children. Don't break apart a family's life just for the money. Besides, this man is in his late fifties, how could he marry someone who could be his grandchild's age? You better refuse this and respect yourself. We might not have a lot of money, but we have dignity."

And so Farima's father worked up the courage to face my father and turn down his "offer." He was outraged.

"Now even if you die I will not give you your money. It's your greed that brought you this trouble."

Two days later, Farima's family received a call from my mother. They were very surprised, not expecting her to know what had happened and then assuming that she was calling to thank them for saving her marriage. But instead she called them filthy names and hung up on them.

They later discovered that my father had told my mother that Farima's family had introduced him to a very beautiful lady to persuade him to marry her. However, he said that he only had eyes for her and would not betray her and their children for some gold diggers who wanted to ruin his reputation.

I asked why her father didn't take legal action. Farima explained that in the purchase agreement papers it said in the fine print that payment installments were not linked to construction milestones.

Having hired some of the best lawyers available to prepare these onerous sales agreements, my father was able to charge and receive payments every six months without ever laying a brick. The whole situation had affected Farima's father's mental state and was straining what had been a happy, strong and solid 40-year marriage to her mother. She was very worried about her father, who was becoming more and more depressed.

Hoping to offer some hope to my friend, I said that her father's money would likely be in an escrow account where it would be safeguarded by a third party until the building project had been completed.

However, Farima said that escrow regulations weren't instituted in Dubai until 2008, almost three years after my father sold most of his real estate projects.

I knew that she spoke the truth. Anger, disappointment and disgust filled my heart.

Wanting to find out more about my father's business operations, I contacted Amir, a young Iranian man who had helped market my father's real estate to expatriates, particularly those living in the large Iranian community in Dubai. Since he was no longer my father's employee, I thought he might be able to speak freely about his experience with the company.

He said that my father's real estate marketing methods were very unprofessional. As demand for a particular real estate project increased, he instructed his sales associates to steadily increase the price. However, toward the end, after they had sold thousands of apartments, demand diminished and he told them not to refuse any price. As a result, buyers paid significantly different prices for the same type of apartment.

In fact, sometimes investors would come across one another by accident and realize that they had both bought the same property. When they went to my father's sales office to complain, Mayed would greet them, explain that it was simply a typing error, and issue them certificates for different units.

Amir told me that sales associates were not allowed to question anything. Those who dared to ask my brothers any questions or to suggest improvements were fired. Many sales associates were hired and then fired after working for only a few days.

What astonished Amir and other sales staff the most was that "Engineer Mustafa", who was presumably in charge of constructing these huge towers, was not even a building engineer. His only experience was in renovating small homes in Ajman. This confirmed my own impressions about the man's qualifications. I think that my father purposely hired a fake engineer because he did not plan on building the towers in the first place. For a fee, "Engineer Mustafa" had agreed to let my father use his name and reputation to provide some legitimacy to his scheme. Then, once the sales were completed, my father was able to dispose of him easily with no questions asked.

Doing further research, I discovered that a number of disgruntled investors had posted their comments online. I learned that my father had engaged an "arbitration company," which I believe was a shadow company and probably owned by my brothers or sisters-in-law, to mediate between my father and dissatisfied investors to settle the latter's accounts. The arbitrator would persuade the investors to agree to receive only 30 percent of what they had paid for the property and to then abandon their case. Otherwise, pressing charges against my father would cost them a great deal in legal costs and would involve extensive waiting times. Moreover, the plaintiffs were unlikely to win the case because my father could afford to retain the best lawyers. My father used every legal loophole and business trick at his disposal to avoid refunding his investors.

Every morning, when I looked at the newspaper, I read articles about my father. They were no longer about his wonderful buildings or latest offerings. They were about his appalling crimes and shameful actions. I read accounts of how he had taken many people's life savings and had given them nothing but pain and poverty. Having initially been told that construction was going according to schedule and would be finished in 2007, these rather naïve investors kept making regular payments.

However, when years passed and they found out that my father had not even started any projects, some of these angry and devastated people began sharing their stories with the media. Others formed action groups and complained to the Real Estate Regulatory

Authority or RERA in Dubai, as reported in one of the local newspapers with the headline, "Disgruntled Investors Storm RERA Office."

Here are some of the stories that came to light.

A middle-aged Filipino expatriate had worked hard for ten years to accrue a small nest egg for himself and his wife and children. When he heard that he could be a homeowner in Dubai, he placed his life savings as a down payment on a two-bedroom apartment. Every day, he and his family dreamt that one day they would finally have a place to call home. When they discovered the painful reality that they had lost all their money and had no home, their dream became a nightmare. It almost destroyed his family.

A young Egyptian man had left his family and homeland to work in Dubai. When he heard about my father's remarkable offerings, he took his savings, obtained a large loan from the bank, and paid my father 1.7 million Dhs for a two-bedroom apartment. He yearned for the day when he would marry and bring his wife to his dream home. But instead he lost his money, his savings, his home, and his hopes for a happy future. His heavy debts put his life on hold for two years. Buried in debt and with no home, he was forced to rent a place and start over.

A woman from India had purchased an office in what was supposed to be a 64-story office building. On her daily visits to father's office, my brother Mayed would greet her with a big smile and offer her refreshments and compliments, but not much else. After she had made payments adding up to more than 700,000 Dhs, Mahed's flattery dissolved and he treated her terribly.

She pleaded for her money back, but of course she didn't succeed.

A British citizen had spent the money that he had inherited from his father on one of my father's fictitious apartments. Accounts of tragedies such as his were no longer confined to local media but soon found their way to international attention, and in fact were featured in "Dubai Dreams," an episode of *Homes from Hell*, a British television documentary series produced by ITV Studios.

Local buyers not only suffered financial losses but worse, their trust was betrayed. For example, an Iranian woman living in Dubai had bought two apartments in one of my father's towers, thinking that because he was a well-respected local businessman, there would be no chance of fraud. But she eventually learned that she was very wrong.

I was ashamed to even say my family name. I could feel anger in the air. My family's victims would blame me for ruining their lives because I was the daughter of a criminal. What they did not know was that I myself was a victim of my own family.

CHAPTER 23

FACE TO FACE

Are you not ashamed of caring so much for the making of money and for fame and prestige, when you neither think nor care about wisdom and truth and the improvement of your soul?
- Socrates

I had always suffered discrimination in my family, but had consoled myself with the thought that at least I had a family. Surely that was worth something. But after I was no longer welcome at their home, a pleasure that had made me look forward to weekends with excitement and had given me a feeling of home and belonging, I realized that I had been deceiving myself.

I also realized that I was not alone in having been mistreated by my family. I began to feel that I had to speak up for others and myself. How long was I going to pretend that everything was going fine when it wasn't? How long was I going to turn a blind eye and let so many people suffer in silence because I was too afraid to speak the truth? How long was I going to live in the shadow of my parents' greed? It was time I faced the fears that had haunted me since childhood. I had been trying for years to run away from them. But I came to realize that if I didn't do something, my fears would chase me for the rest of my life.

I could no longer live with discrimination and injustice. I could no longer stand there and watch people's lives burn to ashes, while my heart burned in sadness. It was time I faced my father.

One weekend morning, I drove alone to my parents' place. On my way from Al Ain to Dubai, memories of my life in that family played in my mind like a movie. Recalling how my parents had treated me and others for all of those years brought anger to my soul. Convinced that what I was about to do was the right thing, I gathered up my strength for the moment that I would face them.

When I arrived at their gate, I was surprised to see a newly constructed guardhouse. Usually, my parents' house gates were wide open, but not any more. When I rang the bell, a tiny window slid open and a man with a deep voice asked, "What do you want?"

"I want to speak to my parents. I am their daughter."

"Sorry. Not allowed."

I insisted that I would not leave until I saw my parents. Finally, after he obtained my father's consent, he unlocked the gates.

Walking down the path toward my parents' doorstep, I saw two more guards dressed in black police hats, light blue shirts and dark blue pants, staring at me as if I was a criminal. I did my best to ignore them and to calm myself down so that I could express myself clearly to my parents. Looking through their French door, I saw them sitting on the sofa and drinking tea. I knocked twice, but they kept on sipping their tea, so I walked in, greeted them, and received a cold, annoyed response.

"Since when do I have to get a guard's permission to see you?"

My mother responded that they probably did not

know who I was because they had never seen me before.

When I asked why they felt the need for bodyguards, she said that since my father had become a very rich and famous man, many poor people wandered into their house and bothered them for money. She also said that Sameera had become even crazier and they feared that she would harm her children.

Although I knew that my parents just wanted to shield themselves from the crowd of angry victims who wanted their money back, I pretended to believe her. I then asked why they had been treating me coldly, especially in the past couple of weeks.

At that point, my father looked directly at me with fire in his eyes and said, "If you wish to visit our house and country estate, you must keep your mouth shut. Don't stick your nose into any of our business and don't ask any more of your stupid questions. I think you know exactly what I mean. Otherwise, consider leaving for good."

At that moment, memories rushed into my mind. I remembered when I was asking Abdul Salam about their business. I felt a chill in my heart. Could someone have been watching me the whole time?

My father's angry gaze reminded me of how he had beaten me as a child. That painful past froze my soul as it often had before, but this time I was not going to let it control me. Somehow I managed to muster up my strength and pass through the gauntlet of fear.

"Father, let me tell you something for the first time—and it could be the last time. But at least for once, please listen to me. I remember just like it was yesterday, when you were lying on the hospital bed shivering from illness. You promised that if God gave you just one more life, you would transform yourself into a better person. God has heard you and has accepted your prayers, blessing you with another life. Not only once, or twice, but three times. When your heart was not functioning properly and death almost had you, God gave you another chance. When you were going to be blind, no longer seeing the beauty and colors of life, my husband saved you and God blessed you with hope. You promised to build a hospital to help the less fortunate, but now you are slowly killing them. You promised to help the poor, but now you are robbing them. You promised to become a better Muslim, but now you are using Islam to cover your dirty works. You promised to help the needy, but now you are feeding off their money. Instead of raising your sons to make a positive influence in society, you discouraged them from getting an education and the only thing they have learned is how to become thieves. The -".

My mother suddenly interrupted me and loudly and furiously yelled, "SHUT UP! Shut it! Keep your mouth shut! You grew to be a very rude person. Your heart is always dark and black. I know that since you were a child you always envied your brothers. You are jealous. You see that we have money and you don't so your bitterness makes you want to ruin our good fortune."

I asked her to please let me finish. I then turned to my father and told him that he thinks he is rich and successful but this will not last forever. He thinks that all the people he stole from will grieve in silence but he is wrong. Justice will eventually rise and destroy him in the end. All the cries of the poor people will haunt him.

But my father had had enough.

"GET OUT! A girl like you should be executed! God and I will never be happy with you in your entire life or afterlife!"

My mother immediately stood up, signaling her hands towards the door.

"OUT! Get up and go out! I wish you had died before you were born!"

I stood up with my head down and left their house. Hearing the loud slam as my mother slammed her French door, my heart shattered into pieces.

I did not know whether my actions were right or wrong. Only time would reveal the true answer. But despite my heartbreak, I felt a sense of bravery and accomplishment for having fought my fears, for having spoken truth to power, for having done what I had wanted to do for so long.

But despite that, I was unable to sleep peacefully. Nightmares haunted my nights. A couple of days later, I phoned my parents and siblings, to see if I still had any standing in my family. My sister, Ghalia, was the only one who responded. She told me that she could no longer talk to me. Otherwise my parents would cut off her monthly allowance and treat her the way they had treated me. She told me that this would be the last time she would speak to me. She meant what she said.

Days turned to weeks and weeks crawled to months and not a single family member called me or asked about me. Every one of them had abandoned me, leaving me to believe that I had done something terrible, that I had betrayed them irrevocably.

I became weak, lost, and depressed. Feeling like a

dark grey thundercloud that had broken into torrents of rain, I collapsed into an emotional breakdown. There was not a single ray of light in my life during the dark, lonely months that followed.

One night I dreamt that I was alone in the middle of the desert. Suddenly, a big vicious wolf came toward me with the clear intent to attack. Sweat ran down my face and fear crept up my spine. I looked around and saw nothing except my parent's house and so, with the wolf right behind me, I ran there as fast as I could. When I finally made it, barely able to catch my breath, the gates closed and locked in front of me. I banged and banged at the gate, weeping in terror. Then I looked up and saw my family standing in their balcony and watching me with serious looks on their faces. The wolf got closer and closer. As it leaped at me, I leapt into wakefulness.

CHAPTER 24

FAREWELL TO MY HOMELAND

Often transformation cannot begin wthout our willingness to liberate ourselves from what's impeding our growth and happiness.
— Gail McMeekin

Time soon revealed the consequences of having faced my parents. I received several calls from relatives after that fateful day. Some of my cousins told me that they had heard about my terrible and rude attitude toward my parents because of my jealousy. They reminded me that my mother had suffered to carry me in her womb for nine months and had brought me into this world. That my parents had fed me, taught me, cared for me, wed me and had bought me a townhouse. They berated me for treating my parents with malice instead of rewarding them with gratitude. They maintained that I had turned against all of the blessings that my family had bestowed upon me, that I had ignored all of their good traits because I only had eyes for the bad. They demanded that I go to them and apologize.

Some of my elderly aunts had even stronger words. They told me that on the day I was taken for burial I would be burning in the fires of hell. Even the graveyard would not want someone like me. They said that if my own parents weren't happy with me, God wouldn't be happy either. How could I have said such things to these angels? They never missed a prayer, never skipped a *Haj* trip, never neglected to fast. They advised me to beg for mercy and to pray that my parents would forgive me.

Even my Aunt Munira called to say that she didn't want any further discussion about her inheritance rights. She didn't want to expose herself to the kind of public mockery that I was subjected to.

At first, I tried to explain to my relatives who my parents really were. But no one wanted to listen, nor did they want to believe. Instead they looked down on me and gossiped about me.

In our society, the majority will take the side of the wealthy in such instances. It did not matter whether they were right or wrong. And in our culture, when people were as close to God as my parents were believed to be, no one would doubt their actions or their faith. I just remained silent, hoping time would soon tell the truth. Meanwhile, their harmful words were soul-destroying.

Early one morning, when I was driving my three kids to school, my mind was preoccupied with negative thoughts arising from the unkind words and the sense of injustice and isolation that I was feeling. I drove along Al Ain's crowded main street, not noticing the roundabout in front of me and I kept on driving without giving the right-of-way to the white car in front of me. With a loud crash, I rear-ended the car and it began spinning around.

Sweat pouring down my face, I stepped on the brake, and I turned to check on my children. Thank God they were fine. I immediately opened the door to see what had happened. The car belonged to another mother who was driving her two young children to school. I apologized and asked her if she and her kids were OK.

She said, "Thank God yes." Although relieved, I still felt terrible.

The negative thoughts were harming not only me, but also my children and other people. But there was nothing I could do, it seemed. There was no way I could release the frustration and anxiety that I was feeling. I was constantly second-guessing my choice to take a stand against my parents' criminal behavior. Filled with regret and guilt for having broken our traditions, part of me was convinced that I was mistaken and that everyone else was right. I wished that I had never opened my mouth and had never stood up against my family. However, another part of me assured me that there was no wrong in doing the right thing – I had simply tried to protect my rights and those of others.

Unable to bear my mental anguish, I went to a psychiatrist. After a thorough diagnosis, he informed me that my depression was a consequence of my traumatic childhood. He explained that since I was no longer in denial as to its harshness, I was overcome by terrible memories that were impossible to handle. He prescribed antidepressants, but those small pills could not solve my big problems. Life became dull and dreary. I lost my passion for doing what I loved and I didn't feel that I took proper care of the people I loved. I started eating more, trying to escape my pain. But all I was really doing was eating up my life.

After a few days, I received a call from my Aunt Latifa. A reticent, helpful woman in her fifties, she did not reproach me as the others had. Instead, having heard about my accident, she wanted to know how I was doing. I told her that my children and I hadn't been hurt, but I was devastated that my parents had not only abandoned me but had also made me out to be a traitor to our family.

I'll never forget her reply: "If you truly knew your family's history, you would not be surprised by what they are doing today."

She explained how my father had made his first fortune in the early 1970s. Since he only had a grade six education, he wasn't able to rise above a very low-ranking position at the bank where he was working, and so he asked his father to find him a better-paying job. My paternal grandfather knew of Karam, a distant relative who had made a lot of money shipping goods from Dubai to India, and he persuaded him to hire Hamad to ship goods for him. However, in reality, Karam was mainly in the business of smuggling gold.

Due to a relatively easy and open border, there were numerous ways to smuggle and ship gold. Carrying along binoculars and a rifle for protection, smugglers like my father became very skilled at hiding gold among food and clothing shipments. My father took blocks of gold to buyers in India, who paid him a good sum of money. Then he would return to Karam with the promised money and receive his own share. After gaining Karam's trust, my father made a large shipment, but this time he did not deliver the gold to the usual customers, but instead sold it to other buyers. The regular customers were furious and were determined to punish and perhaps kill him for betraying them. My father hid in India for a while before secretly returning to Dubai with a large sum of money. This time, he did not give any of it to Karam. Since gold smuggling was illegal, Karam could not launch a formal complaint against him. To this day, he is not on speaking terms with my father.

After learning the ins and outs of the trade and establishing a working relationship with the new gold smugglers, my father decided to operate his own gold smuggling business. He used some of his profits to buy a large wooden cargo ship, which he named after Sultan. He also hired Indian workers to ship the gold for him. Each time he did this, he made large amounts of money, until one day his ship was caught and confiscated by the Indian Coast Guard. That was the end of my father's gold smuggling days.

I couldn't believe what I was hearing. I asked her why she hadn't spoken up about this sooner. She replied that she was not the only family member who knew about my father's criminal background, and that in fact some knew more than her. But everyone was afraid to open the door of trouble when there was no benefit behind it.

Also, if anyone so much as hinted at how they had obtained their money, my family would destroy that person's life. After hearing a few nasty rumors and lies from my mother and others, the community would look upon them with different eyes. In addition, a number of people had their own dark secrets. If they were to divulge my family's misdeeds, my parents would counterattack by exposing the skeletons in their closets. Nobody wanted to have his or her reputation damaged. Aunt Latifa said that she hadn't wanted to ruin my relationship with my parents and wouldn't have told me any of this if I hadn't been suffering.

I pleaded with her to tell me more about my father. She then told me the story of her uncle, a very old man in his eighties who was nearly blind. He owned a small old building located on Dubai's main street. One day, my father invited him to his country estate, where he showed him a document that presumably conveyed a warning that the government was going to take away his building if he did not demolish the old one and build a new one. Her uncle was petrified of losing his only building simply because he did not have the money to fix it. So my father offered to buy the old building from him so that he wouldn't need to stress about it anymore. Her uncle was very thankful and, although unable to read it, signed the offered agreement. However, after a while, he came to realize that he had been deceived and that my father had paid him less than a quarter of the property's market value. Feeling old, blind, and helpless, he cried every night about this depressing turn of events. No matter how hard Latifa tried to convince him to move on with his life, he was unable to do so. Seeing her elderly uncle crying broke her heart, but she could not press charges against my father because her uncle had signed a binding agreement. He lived in misery until his death.

She also informed me that my father had stolen not only from people in Dubai, but also from investors in the Philippines. He had sent Sultan and Margie there to employ the same criminal tactics that they had used here. Now they were wanted on fraud charges and would never be able to travel there again.

From delaying each court case as much as possible to discouraging the victims from pursuing their rights, my father used a number of tactics to evade justice. He tried to make it so expensive for plaintiffs to proceed with their cases that they would be discouraged from pressing charges against him. Sometimes he intimidated investors by cancelling their visas if they continued to pursue their cases. On those rare occasions when investors were still determined to proceed, my father would promise to pay their money in installments, which of course he never did. Another of his tricks was to bribe some of the authorities to ignore the filed cases.

At the end of 2008, during the global financial crisis, Hamad blamed the global recession for not delivering on his real estate sales or for not refunding the investors' money. However, in reality, all of his projects were supposed to have been delivered by 2007.

The global financial crisis was a global glory for him. It was a great excuse for him not to refund the investors and also to ask the banks to extend the terms of their loans. It is likely that hundreds of millions of *dirhams* were transferred either to his or my mother's foreign bank accounts. Some of the investors' money was also diverted toward his own real estate projects such as his skyscraper on Sheikh Zayed Street.

I also heard that he advised my brothers and their wives not to display their extravagant lifestyles in public. In addition, he changed his businesses to *limited liability companies (LLC)*, so that the people suing him wouldn't have access to his personal wealth.

But his most effective strategy was to do what he had always done best – to hide behind the shield of religion as a man of God, hoping people would see him as a pure and innocent old man. He increased the frequency of his holy visits to Mecca and would simply say that he did not know what was going on in his business.

I came to see my father as an unhappy man, despite all of his assets. Years of deception, lies, secrecy and hypocrisy had taken their toll on his physical health and emotional wellbeing. Although he became increasingly rich in material possessions, he became increasingly poor in his morals, principles, and personal integrity.

I saw my mother as a heartless hunter who didn't care how she got her money. The only thing she cared about was being able to brag about her luxurious lifestyle in order to gain some respect in her community.

Looking at my brothers, I saw no brotherly love, compassion or understanding among them. The only thing they shared was a desire to extort money, especially from the poor and vulnerable. The only thing they had learned in life was how to steal using different fraudulent schemes and how to cover them up.

Money had blinded all of them and had taken over their lives.

Gradually, depression was taking over my life, bringing pain to my body and despair to my soul. I cried frequently, often for no apparent reason. I saw the world as a dark place. The food I ate had no taste. The places I saw had no color. The sleep I slept had no dreams. The thoughts I thought had no optimism. And the problems I suffered had no answers. Day by day, my weight increased. The things that used to bring joy to my heart now brought nothing but indifference. The clock would be ticking every second but, to me, it stayed in one place forever. I would wake up to a dark morning, live a sad day and sleep a sleepless night. I felt as though I was living a slow death. How would I escape this pain? When I looked in the mirror, I saw a woman I had never known: an overweight, sick, depressed, lonely and hopeless mother. It had been a year and a half of misery since confronting my parents and I could no longer endure it.

In desperation, I asked my husband to take me back to Canada. I hoped I would feel better there. After a few weeks of long discussion, my husband finally agreed to leave the job that he loved. I was truly touched by his decision. We decided that, at the end of the 2010 academic year, we would move to Canada. I counted the days and nights until the time came for us to leave this place and my painful memories.

The night before I left, I decided to call my parents. I wanted to say good-bye for good, hoping they would answer my call, at least for the last time. When I phoned my father, he did not answer, but my mother did.

"I'm just calling to tell you that I will be going back to Canada for good tomorrow. I am calling to say good-bye."

"Can you do me a favor?" she asked.

I felt excited when she said that. Despite all the cruel things that she had done to me, I held out hope that she would ask me to stay because she would miss me.

"Don't ever come back again," she ordered, "Your place in our lives is dead. Your days in our family are over."

That was our last conversation.

The last night was the longest night of my life. It was as though the alarm clock would never move and the sun would never rise. Terrible memories flooded through my mind. Finally, the clock went off at 3:00 AM. It was not yet dawn when we took a taxi to Dubai International Airport.

As the airplane slowly took off, I looked out the window. Dawn was just breaking in the pink sky while tiny orange lights sparkled on the ground of my country. As we ascended, a tear slid down my face. I was leaving my country, not knowing if I would ever return.

As my homeland disappeared from view, I didn't know whether or not my decision was a good one, but what I did know was that I didn't want my children, or any other woman or child, to suffer as I had. Despite my shattered heart, I also knew that no matter how dark the night, the sun of justice will eventually rise. And no matter how muted our voices, they will eventually break free, louder and stronger, for the whole world to hear.

Epilogue

One thing that my experience has impressed upon me is the importance of education. Witnessing my family's behavior, I have seen that, to the uneducated, richness is defined by material possessions, power is achieved by stepping on others, and status is measured by the number of boys in their household. Within that worldview, life has no greater purpose than pursuing and amassing money.

I am grateful to have had the opportunity to see that education can inspire us to become more capable parents, more engaged citizens, and more resourceful human beings. Knowledge has the power to widen our eyes, open our minds, and enable us to see past people's gender or economic status. It can help us value pricelessness over price tag. It can help us recognize the shame in humiliating and the grace in humility. And it can help us to understand that there is no greater richness than love.

Let us call the world to come together – every child, every woman and every man. Let us draw a bigger picture, one that enters every home, every heart and brings together every voice.

Let us listen to the helpless cries of the abused and neglected children. Let us listen more deeply to women who are being abused, blamed and discriminated against, while trapped in cages of injustice, fear and shame, with no option but to suffer in silence.

Let us transform all the voices and sounds of hopelessness into a beautiful melody that plays to the world. The birds will sing our stories. Rainbows will dazzle with color in a sky that is no longer grey.

GLOSSARY

Abaya A simple, loose robe-like dress or cloak worn by some women in parts of the Islamic world. Sometimes referred to as aba, the traditional abaya is black and covers the whole body except for the face, feet, and hands.

Ajman The United Arab Emirates' smallest emirate (260 sq km or 100 sq mi).

Al Ain The second largest city in the Emirate of Abu Dhabi and the fourth largest city in the United Arab Emirates. Also known as "The Garden City" because of its greenery, it is located approximately 160 km east of the capital city, Abu Dhabi, and about 130 km south of Dubai. The literal translation of Al Ain is "The Eye."

Al Karama Sometimes referred to as Karama, it is part of the bustling older section of the city of Dubai and is a popular place to shop for bargains.

Allah Akbar The Muslim call to prayer, or *adhan*. Its usual translation is "God is the greatest."

Angioplasty A surgical technique that involves inserting a collapsed balloon into a narrowed or obstructed blood vessel and then inflating it. To ensure that the vessel remains open, a stent, or mesh tube, may be inserted at the time of ballooning.

Baklava A dessert consisting of layers of filo pastry filled with chopped nuts and sweetened with syrup or honey.

Basbousa A sweet cake made of semolina or farina soaked in syrup, which may contain orange flower water or rose water. Coconut is a popular addition.

Dirhams (AED) The currency of the United Arab Emirates, valued at .27 USD (12/10/12). Informal abbreviations are DH or Dhs.

Eid Al-Adha Translated as "Festival of Sacrifice" or "Greater Eid," this is an important religious holiday celebrated by Muslims worldwide to commemorate the willingness of Abraham (Ibrahim) to sacrifice his son Ishmael as an act of obedience to Allah. Allah, however, intervened and provided him with a lamb to sacrifice instead.

Gangrene A potentially life-threatening condition that arises when a large mass of body tissue dies, perhaps after an injury or infection, or as a consequence of a chronic health condition affecting blood circulation such as diabetes.

Haj A pilgrimage to the Holy City of Mecca made during the 12th and final month in the Islamic calendar. The Haj is a religious duty that must be carried out at least once in the lifetime of every able-bodied Muslim who can afford it. It is a demonstration of the solidarity of the Muslim people and of their submission to God.

Harrees (Harissa) A Middle Eastern dish consisting of cracked or coarsely ground wheat mixed with beef, lamb, or chicken.

Ihram (Ahram) Clothing worn by Muslims during the Haj. Men's garments consist of two white sheets of fabric (usually toweling material). The top is draped over the torso and a belt secures the bottom sheet. Women's clothing varies considerably and reflects regional as well as religious influences.

Jebel Hafeet A mountain on the outskirts of Al Ain in the United Arab Emirates. It straddles part of the border between the Emirate of Abu Dhabi and the Sultanate of Omar.

Limited Liability Company (LLC) A type of company that affords its principals with limited liability for the company's debts and actions.

Niqab A cloth that covers the face.

Prayer beads A string of 33 or 99 beads used by Muslims to count their repetitions of prayers, chants, or invocations *(Dhikr)*.

Prayer rug A mat or piece of fabric to keep the worshiper clean and comfortable during prayer.

Ramadan A 29 to 30-day period of fasting that occurs in the ninth month of the Islamic calendar. Intended to teach Muslims about patience, spirituality, humility, and surrender to God, participating Muslims refrain from eating or drinking during daylight hours.

Retinal detachment An eye disorder in which the retina peels away from its underlying layer of support tissue. Without rapid treatment, the entire retina may detach, resulting in vision loss and most likely blindness.

Sepsis A potentially deadly medical condition characterized by a whole-body inflammation that is triggered by an infection.

Shawarma A meat preparation in which lamb, goat, chicken, turkey, beef, or mixed meats are placed on a spit and grilled for as long as a day. Shavings are then cut off the block of meat and served with accompaniments such as hummus, salad, and other vegetables. Shawarma also refers to a pita bread sandwich or wrap made with shawarma meat.

Zamzam water Sourced from the Zamzam well, which is located within *Masjid al-Haram,* Mecca's largest mosque, it is considered by devout Muslims to be miraculously generated water from God.

About the Author

Fourteen-year-old Maha Al Fahim is passionate about the role of education in ending social ills such as child abuse and discrimination. She is an honor roll student and a student council president at her school. A tireless volunteer, Maha has tutored children with special needs, assisted at children's summer camps, helped seniors and the homeless, and has taken a leadership role in an organization promoting cycling in her community. She is also a committed practitioner of Kung Fu, a member of Team Canada 2014 for martial arts, and was a gold medal winner at the 2014 World Martial Arts Games.

A lover of theatre and ballet, Maha is active in her school's creative writing program and loves writing poems and essays. This is her first book.

Made in the USA
San Bernardino, CA
27 April 2018